POETS

IN THEIR

PRIDE

BASIC BOOKS, INC., PUBLISHERS
New York

POETS
in Their
PRIDE

GEOFFREY GRIGSON

à Victoria, ce petit livre des
poètes du pays natal de son père

PREFACE

Poets are proud people, who try to defeat time.

Most of us live and die and do not leave much behind (except perhaps a million pounds or dollars in a will, or a million minus nine-hundred and ninety thousand). Thomas Hardy, one of the twelve poets described in this book, wrote about going into a churchyard and hearing speech among the graves from the dead who are going to die the second death, when people forget them, when "memory of them numbs."

This sounds gloomy, but poets are different, poets live and are life, and are not forgotten, unless they are shams. Or if they do die that second death, it comes after a very long while, only after centuries, when their country dies or their language dies out.

So poets are naturally proud; which is not the same as conceited. In other ways, they are often the most humble and unassuming people. You cannot usually tell them, for example, by their dress or their hair style. If someone says with contempt, "he looks like a poet," he shares a wrong idea that the poets are typically pale and wear arty clothes, and seldom clean their nails.

Poets are extraordinary, but not in that way as a rule, though I admit that Tennyson liked to be photographed in grand poetic poses. In everyday life it was Tennyson's strength and size and handsomeness which made him look different, not his "artiness."

In this book I have chosen twelve favorite poets of mine to exhibit in their pride and in their courage, another quality that distinguishes the poet. Each one knew that he had an exceptional power of using words so that they stay "alive" and affect other people. Each one felt that his English words, built up into poems in this way, could make a fool of time. Each one had the poet's ability to be "true" now and again.

That is to say that each had the gift of making something no one else could make, without imitation, without obeying a fashion, without bothering about critics ("Why will not my subjects write in brose?" asked George III, who couldn't pronounce English very well), and without currying favor.

But it is no good talking about poets minus their poems. So a few poems follow each of these twelve chapters, which are about poets who wrote and lived in the long space of four centuries, from the sixteenth century to our own.

Geoffrey Grigson

CONTENTS

ILLUSTRATIONS

And give our labours yet this poor delight,
   That when our days do end they are not done;
And though we die, we shall not perish quite,
   But live two lives, where others have but one.

Samuel Daniel

POETS

IN THEIR

PRIDE

Sir Philip Sidney
Gallery

Detail from the painting in the National Portrait

ONE

Sir Philip Sidney
(*1554-1586*)

Few poets are poets all the time. They do other things. Caedmon kept pigs, Chaucer was a diplomat, Villon a burglar, Marlowe a spy, Shakespeare an actor, Vaughan a country doctor, Milton a civil servant, Blake an engraver, Clare a laborer, Christina Rossetti a governess, Matthew Arnold an inspector of schools; Hardy was an architect and a novelist, Gerard Manley Hopkins was a priest, Walt Whitman edited newspapers, T. S. Eliot worked in a bank and then became a publisher, W. H. Auden was a schoolmaster.

There is no "art-uniform" by which you can recognize poets. Their peculiarity is inside them. Most of them write poems in between whiles; and if you need a definition of poetry, I shall say that poems are made of words in a special state of being together: a poem is words which a poet likes, put together in his way, his "style," and a proper shape or form, prompted by something which particularly moved him and possessed him.

All of this fits Sir Philip Sidney. Poetry moved him from childhood. When he was a boy he had heard a blind harper in the Midlands singing the ballad of "The Hunting of the Cheviot"; he had found his heart "moved more than with a trumpet," and had sent the harper a shilling by his servant.

But he never liked to think of himself as only a poet: he wanted to be much else, a man of learning, a diplomat, a statesman, a soldier, a promoter of exploration, a man who did things rather than one who sat still and watched.

Then there came to him, when he was twenty-six, before he had done half the things he wished to do, a fire of emotion which seemed to burn up his life and which made words, words, and more words join together in more than a hundred special poems. The fire was the loss of the girl he expected to marry, Penelope Devereux, eighteen years old, a girl with tenderness and grace, a pink and white skin, black and very lively eyes, and blonde hair, who was now to be married against her inclination to Lord Rich.

Lord Rich, though rich decidedly, was a brute and a bully and a fool. Philip Sidney was a lark rising with the sun: he was "mild," gay, clever, good, and good-looking, with an astonishing power to make everyone he met love him and admire him. But he was poor by the standards of great Tudor noblemen; and his family, once favored by Queen Mary, whose husband King Philip of Spain had been his godfather, and had given him his Christian name, was not much in favor with Queen Elizabeth.

Sidney had grown up in the wide, low, still existing mansion of Penshurst Place, in Kent (not far from Tunbridge Wells), where he had been born in 1554, and since his father was Lord President of the Marches of Wales and lived in official state away at Ludlow Castle, he had been taken from Kent when he was ten and sent to school at Shrewsbury, not far from Ludlow, among the narrow blue hills of the Welsh border. Later on his sister, patroness of poets, Shakespeare included, married the Earl of Pembroke and went to live at Wilton House, under Salisbury Plain, in Wiltshire, where Sidney wrote many of his poems.

So Kent, Shropshire, and Wiltshire were Sidney's counties.

At Shrewsbury even his schoolmasters had admired his charm and sweetness and good sense. When he was seventeen his father had sent him abroad for two years, after he left the university. When he was twenty-two the Queen had sent him abroad again as a special envoy.

> . . . all mens hearts with secret ravishment
> He stole away.

Kings, princes, scholars, poets, philosophers, all of them had realized, though he was so young, that they had never met so perfect a man. In the Netherlands (where he was to die), he had been received by the famous Don John of Austria, the Spanish Viceroy. Another poet, his friend Fulke Greville, described how this haughty, most noble enemy unbent to him. "At the first, in his Spanish haughture, he gave him access as by descent to a youth, of grace as to a stranger, and in particular competition (as he conceived) to an enemy; yet after a while that he had taken his just altitude, he found himself so stricken with this extraordinary Planet, that the beholders wondered to see what ingenuous tribute that brave and high minded Prince paid to his worth; giving more honour and respect to this hopefull young Gentleman, than to the Embassadors of mighty Princes."

Fulke Greville, who had been at school at Shrewsbury with this young Philip Sidney, wrote that he was Zephyrus, the gentle west wind, "giving life where he blew." Also that he was one of those rare men whose "heart and tongue went one way," and that to his active spirit "all depths of the Devill proved but shallow fords."

It was among those comings and goings, when the greatest things were expected of him, and when he was growing up to be the hero of a generation, that he met Penelope Devereux, daughter of the Earl of Essex. They may have seen each other first when Queen Elizabeth, with Sidney in her train, was received by Penelope's mother at Chartley Castle, in Staffordshire, in 1575. But Penelope was then only twelve, to Sidney's twenty-one. "Not at the first sight," Sidney wrote afterward in a poem, "Love gave the wound, which while I breathe, will bleed." He came gradually into love, seeing more and more of her in London, as she grew up.

Penelope's father had been ravished by him, like everyone else, old or young. And though he was not wealthy, there was more than Philip Sidney's celebrity and attractiveness to make him a possible husband: he was heir to the great Earl of Leicester, who was his uncle; and when Penelope's father was dying of a sudden illness in 1576, he said that he wished Philip Sidney and Penelope might marry.

Then Penelope's mother married again—married this Earl of Leicester; they had a son, and Philip Sidney was heir no longer, and a possible match no longer.

Quickly, decisively, with no argument, Penelope Devereux was married off to her young, detested, very wealthy and on that account so very suitable Lord Rich.

She came back to court as another man's wife, and the poems began. Sidney was now "straw set on fire" by her black eyes. She had not been exactly in love with him before her marriage; nor had Sidney been altogether in love with her, but now he realized what he had lost. She was both aloof and touched, then both loving and ungiving. "As good to write, as for to lie and groan": in the poems, the songs, the sonnets, one after another, Sidney painted his hell.

He wrote of seeing her, touching her, lacking her; he wrote of the wind in her blonde hair as she was rowed on the Thames. He wrote of his success in a tournament, before the queen and the French ambassador, because *she* was watching. He wrote of kissing her. She was "Stella" or the Star, he was Astrophel, meaning the one who loved a star:

4

When I say Stella, I do mean the same
   Princess of Beauty, for whose only sake
   The rains of love I love, though never slake,
   And joy therein, though nations count it shame.

At first he had not known the kind of poem to write, the kind of master to follow, so the words limped and stopped, and older love poems by other poets were obstacles in his way.

Thus, great with child to speak, and helpless in my throes,
   Biting my truant pen, beating my self for spite,
   Fool, said my Muse to me, look in thy heart and write.

He looked and wrote; and said that his "very ink turned straight to Stella's name."

Everything else was dust. Sidney forgot, or pushed away, his public life. He was a man in love, not just a paraded paragon of all the virtues.

He was down, he was up, he was dejected, he was miserable, he was suddenly happy because Penelope was kind, then miserable again, and with no hope, because she drew away. Everything was Penelope—or Stella; was *you, you, you:*

To you, to you, all song of praise is due:
   Only in you my song begins and endeth.

It was hopeless; and great flamings of love, of one-sided love, have in the end to burn down. Then they glow, then the cinders go black, gray, and cold.

But much of this great flaming of love, in 1581, line by line, rhyme by rhyme, keeps burning even now in these poems of "Astrophel and Stella," which Sidney, in the pains of his hell, showed one by one, as he wrote them, to his friends; and which we have been reading ever since.

Sidney went on living. He married, he had children (Penelope, too, accustomed herself to her husband, Lord Rich, and had seven children by him, though she left him later on), he was made Governor of Flushing and General of the Horse in the fighting for the Low Countries against the Spaniards. He died his famous death, after a bullet had broken his thigh bone and plowed along his thigh during an engagement below the walls of the town of Zutphen. Sidney's horse carried him out of the field: "In which sad progress, passing along by the rest of the army . . . and being thirsty with excess of bleeding, he called for drink, which was presently brought him; but as he was putting the bottle to his mouth, he saw a poor Souldier carryed along, who had eaten his last at the same Feast, gastly casting up his eyes at the bottle. Which Sir Philip perceiving, took it from his head, before he drank, and delivered it to the poor man, with these words, *Thy necessity is yet greater than mine.* And when he had pledged this poor souldier, he was presently carried to Arnheim."

There, after sixteen days, his death came from gangrene, on October 17, 1586; the news crossed to England, and everyone was stunned at the passing of the man (he was only thirty-one) who had been the image of all that every educated Englishman of that time wished to be.

His body was taken home in his ship, the "Black Pinnace," which his servants dressed in black sails and black tackling. The Black Pinnace sailed up the Thames, Sidney was carried ashore at the Tower of London, and eleven days later the saddest and grandest procession followed him into Old St. Paul's, which was also draped with black. "It was accounted a sin for any gentleman of quality, for many months after, to appear at Court or City in any light or gaudy apparel."

Sidney's tomb was destroyed in the Fire of London. But if you go to Warwick, in the parish church you can see the tomb of his friend from school to death, Fulke Greville Lord Brooke; it is a severe cold mausoleum of pillars, and pyramids and pinnacles in black and white marble, nearly filling a little chapter-house. Greville had it built while he was still alive, and he allowed only this inscription on it: *Fulke Grevil, Servant to Queene Elizabeth, Councellor to King Iames, and Frend to Sr Philip Sidney. Trophaeum Peccati.* *

Not a word more.

Yet would we, do you think, remember this legend of Philip Sidney, all his wonderful virtues, all his charm, and the famous story of the poor soldier and the cup of water, would we care at all for *Arcadia,* the long romance he wrote for his sister the Countess of Pembroke (now so tiresome to read), or even for his famous essay *The Defence of Poesie,* if Sidney hadn't been the one thing he least valued, a poet?

And if he hadn't written the poems of "Astrophel and Stella," not for fame, he protested, but because he could not help it, because Penelope's beauty had dictated his words, and love had held his hand and made him write?

In *The Defence of Poesie* Sidney said something which is to the point, that poems are stronger or better than nature: "Nature never set forth the earth in so rich tapestry as divers poets have done, neither with pleasant rivers, fruitful trees, sweet-smelling flowers, or whatsoever else may make the too much loved earth more lovely. Her world is brazen, the poets only deliver a golden"—which lasts, and does not rust or discolor.

---

* Monument of a sinner.

YOU THAT DO SEARCH

You that do search for every purling spring
    Which from the ribs of old Parnassus flows,
    And every flower, not sweet perhaps, which grows
    Near thereabouts, into your poesy wring;

Ye that do dictionary's method bring
    Into your rhymes, running in rattling rows;
    You that poor Petrarch's long-deceasèd woes
    With new-born sighs and denizen'd wit do sing;

You take wrong ways; those far-fet helps be such
    As do bewray a want of inward touch,
    And sure at length stol'n goods do come to light:

But if, both for your love and skill, your name
    You seek to nurse at fullest breasts of Fame,
    Stella behold, and then begin to endite.

MY TRUE LOVE HATH MY HEART

My true love hath my heart and I have his,
By just exchange one for another given;
I hold his dear, and mine he cannot miss;
There never was a better bargain driven.
    My true love hath my heart and I have his.

His heart in me keeps him and me in one,
My heart in him his thoughts and senses guides;
He loves my heart, for once it was his own;
I cherish his, because in me it bides.
    My true love hath my heart and I have his.

WITH HOW SAD STEPS, O MOON

With how sad steps, O Moon, thou climb'st the skies,
    How silently, and with how wan a face!
    What may it be, that even in heav'nly place
    That busy archer his sharp arrows tries?

Sure if that long with love acquainted eyes
    Can judge of love, thou feel'st a lover's case;
    I read it in thy looks, thy languisht grace
    To me that feel the like, thy state descries.

Then ev'n of fellowship, O Moon, tell me,
    Is constant love deem'd there but want of wit?
    Are beauties there as proud as here they be?

Do they above love to be lov'd, and yet
    Those lovers scorn whom that love doth possess?
    Do they call virtue there ungratefulness?

STELLA, THINK NOT THAT I

Stella, think not that I by verse seek fame,
    Who seek, who hope, who love, who live but thee;
    Thine eyes my pride, thy lips mine history:
    If thou praise not, all other praise is shame.

Nor so ambitious am I as to frame
    A nest for my young praise in laurel tree:
    In truth, I swear I wish not there should be
    Graved in mine epitaph a Poet's name.

Ne, if I would, could I just title make,
    That any laud thereof to me should grow,
    Without my plumes from others' wings I take:

For nothing from my wit or will doth flow,
    Since all my words thy beauty doth endite,
    And love doth hold my hand, and makes me write.

RING OUT YOUR BELLS

Ring out your bells. Let mourning shows be spread;
For Love is dead:
    All Love is dead, infected
With plague of deep disdain:
    Worth, as nought worth, rejected,
And Faith fair scorn doth gain.
    From so ungrateful fancy,
    From such a female franzy,
    From them that use men thus,
    Good Lord, deliver us!

Weep, neighbours, weep; do you not hear it said
That Love is dead?
    His death-bed, peacock's folly;
His winding sheet is shame;
    His will, false-seeming holy;
His sole exectour, blame.
    From so ungrateful fancy,
    From such a female franzy,
    From them that use men thus,
    Good Lord, deliver us!

Let dirge be sung, and trentals rightly read,
For Love is dead;
    Sir Wrong his tomb ordaineth
My mistress' marble heart,
    Which epitaph containeth,
'Her eyes were once his dart.'
    From so ungrateful fancy,

From such a female franzy,
From them that use men thus,
Good Lord, deliver us!

Alas, I lie: rage hath this error bred;
Love is not dead;
Love is not dead, but sleepeth
In her unmatchèd mind,
Where she his counsel keepeth,
Till due desert she find.
Therefore from so vile fancy,
To call such wit a franzy,
Who Love can temper thus,
Good Lord, deliver us!

SPLENDIDIS LONGUM VALEDICO NUGIS*

Leave me, O Love, which reachest but to dust;
    And thou, my mind, aspire to higher things;
    Grow rich in that which never taketh rust;
    What ever fades, but fading pleasure brings.

Draw in thy beams, and humble all thy might
    To that sweet yoke where lasting freedoms be;
    Which breaks the clouds, and opens forth the light,
    That doth both shine, and give us sight to see.

O take fast hold; let that light be thy guide
    In this small course which birth draws out to death,
    And think how evil becometh him to slide,

Who seeketh heav'n, and comes of heav'nly breath.
    Then farewell, world; thy uttermost I see:
    Eternal Love, maintain thy life in me.

* I bid a long farewell to splendid trifles.

Sir Walter Ralegh   *Detail from the painting in the National Por-trait Gallery*

TWO

Sir Walter Ralegh
(*1552?-1618*)

Sir Walter Ralegh wrote a line in one of his longest poems which put his own view about things into nine words—"Blossoms of pride that can not fade nor fall." He wrote "fade" with a "v," "that can not vade nor fall," since that was how he pronounced it, with a Devonshire accent, for he began life as quite a poor boy in Devonshire (a great county for poets), after which, in all his grandeurs and greatness about the court of Queen Elizabeth, he never lost his West Country speech.

Long after his death, it was remembered that pride had been Sir Walter Ralegh's fault and birth-mark: "He was damnable proud," as poets often are; and he knew it, and knew that the proud have enemies. Being "such a person, every way, that a Prince would rather be afrayd of than ashamed of," pride, in the end, caused his head to be cut off on Tower Hill.

In a way the pride began with the poverty. Walter Ralegh's father in his thatched manor house, set with small Tudor windows (which you can still see at East Budleigh in the red-earthed country of South Devon), had no big estates. But Ralegh (who was born there about 1552) would have grown up to know that his new Elizabethan world was one of great

17

opportunity, if you had ambition enough. He was tall, he was handsome, he moved with grace, he was clever. With his broad Devonshire voice (no one cared about accents) he left the manor house to be a scholar, first of all (at Oxford), then a soldier, then—if he could manage it—a courtier.

Ralegh wished to be everything. He wished to do everything, and to know everybody worth knowing. That was his pride. His wish was to climb into the proudest position at court, to wear with pride clothes grander and more fashionable than anybody else's, to command the proudest wealth, the proudest power over other men. Since this young man, who had an "awfulness and ascendancy in his aspect over other mortals," was also a man of learning, feeling, and imagination, it was his pride as well to become friendly with the most learned men, the most daring thinkers, and the best poets, and to write poems of his own, equal to the finest, which would be read by the Queen, and passed round among the writers and the wits of London. These might be the unfading, unfalling blossoms of his pride.

All was well, to begin with. The Queen liked his spirit, and she made him wealthy. She gave him offices, properties, privileges, she made plain Captain Walter Ralegh, handsome nobody, into Sir Walter Ralegh, Knight. He was the young soldier, after all—or so the story says, and why shouldn't it be true?—who had put down his cloak for the Queen to walk on:

"This captain Ralegh coming out of Ireland"—he had been fighting there—"to the English court in good habit (his clothes being then a considerable part of his estate) found the queen walking, till meeting with a plashy place, she seemed to scruple going thereon. Presently Ralegh cast and spread his new plush cloak on the ground, whereon the queen trod gently, rewarding him afterwards with many suits, for his so free and seasonable tender of so fair a footcloth."

There is another story: that he wrote with a diamond on a glass window:

Fain would I climb, yet fear I to fall

—under which the Queen scratched with her diamond (though she wasn't so good a poet):

If thy heart fails thee, climb not at all.

One thing Queen Elizabeth gave him was a fine mansion on the Strand, in London, on the edge or bank, or precisely the "strand," of the Thames. There this soldier with a good brain and a good wit, this man who "was no Slug" and had without doubt "a wonderfull waking spirit, and a great judgment to guide it," would retreat from his busy life around the court; and in a small study, in one of the turrets, which looked down into the Thames and across the Thames, giving Ralegh the pleasantest and most refreshing of views, he wrote his poems, teasing and building into a whole structure some deep phrase which had come into his head.

He knew courts were dangerous. Coming from a poor house in Devon, with no great family behind him, Ralegh knew that once he had reached the top his happiness might decay, and hatred and envy and malice would abound. Then the odds were that he would die under the axe, like other men who had been favorites.

He thought about who was out and who was in. He wrote poems, in between whiles, precisely about falling from favor, about death and execution, and against the pomps he enjoyed so much—also poems about love, including the idealized love of the Queen, which she expected from her young vigorous courtiers and devotees.

Then love did Ralegh harm as well as good. He was more than ever the Queen's favorite, but he had fallen in love with one of her maids of honor, Mistress Elizabeth Throck-morton. He had married her; and she had borne him a son.

All this was done in secret: secret marriage, secret birth, se-cret christening; and Ralegh's young wife, as though nothing had happened, had gone back to court.

The queen ruled the personal lives of her favorite courtiers, and her maids of honor, so both Ralegh and Elizabeth were certain of the Queen's anger, when she knew. Ralegh had risked all his fortune and future. And when the Queen did know, they both felt her displeasure very quickly. They were imprisoned in the Tower of London, the young mother for several months, Ralegh for several weeks.

Inside the dead walls of the Tower, in despair and feeling his ruin, Ralegh had plenty of time to write—to the Queen— that long poem in which he spoke of the "blossoms of pride that cannot vade nor fall."

But Ralegh was favored no more, he had to leave the court, he had fallen from the crests of fortune, and had taken a step toward his own death.

He was still the man of action, the man of affairs: he ex-plored in South America, sailing to find a gold mine up the Orinoco, he fought the Spaniards. But the Queen died, and the new King James came down from Scotland, and believed easily enough that this damnable proud Ralegh was plotting against him.

So Ralegh found himself back again inside the walls of the Tower, and on trial for his life on a false charge of treason, for which he was most unjustly condemned to death on No-vember 17, 1603. "Thou art an odious fellow," he was told during the trial by the lawyer prosecuting him for the King, "thy name is hateful to all the realm of England for thy pride." It was now in the Tower that he is supposed to have written his poem about his soul's pilgrimage from the block to heaven:

Seeing my flesh must die so soon
And want a head to dine next noon.

He wrote that his soul, "like a white palmer" or pilgrim, would
travel from the block to the land of heaven, over silver mountains and past nectar fountains; and he must have thought
about other deaths, other executions, in which he had had a
part; about other last nights of life (once he had sat through
the night with a Catholic priest who was to die the next day,
arguing with him about the immortality of the soul).

But he was reprieved on December 6th. And now he had
time indeed, thirteen years of it in the Tower, not in darkness
or dungeon, but caged in reasonable comfort, with books, paper, and ink. Prince Henry, the King's son, said: "Only my
father would keep such a bird in a cage."

No longer having to snatch a moment here and there, as
he used to do in his turret study on the Strand, he wrote the
first, grand, melancholy volume of a huge *History of the
World,* ending with a piece on death, who had so often
looked him, one way and another, in the eye:

O eloquent, just, and mighty Death! whom none could
advise, thou has persuaded; what none hath dared thou
hast done; and whom all the world hath flattered thou
only hast cast out of the world and despised: thou hast
drawn together all the far-stretched greatness, all the
pride, cruelty, and ambition of man, and covered it all
over with these two narrow words, Hic Jacet.*

After thirteen years he was let out of the Tower to sail
back to Guinea and up the Orinoco in search of the gold
mine he had seen. He did not find it, his son was killed, he
returned in 1618, in a ship called "Destiny," and straightaway,
on the old verdict of 1603, the King and his enemies had their

* Here lies.

way, and his head was cut from his body on the 29th of October, after he had looked at the axe, tried his finger along its sharpness, and remarked: "It is a sharp and fair medicine to cure me of all my diseases."

The night before he died Ralegh remembered a love poem by himself about a girl of "snow and silk." This girl seems to have been his wife, as she became, his Elizabeth Throckmorton, and he had written it while he was besieging her, without success, some thirty years before. The poem said her beauty framed a heart of stone, and ended with a complaint that Time would make dust of our youth, our joys, our everything.

In his room in the Tower, he now took this last stanza and quickly made it into a poem by itself, altering it a little, but in such a way as to show how much he now agreed, from bitter experience and from the certainty of execution the next day, with what he had felt about Time and Death and the Grave so long before. Then he opened his Bible and wrote the poem out on the flyleaf.

It became known (you will find it on page 27), it went round from mouth to mouth, everyone liking to copy it out for himself.

That is not all. His wife, after his execution, obtained Ralegh's head, with its sharp beard which curled up by nature, as though with natural pride. She had it embalmed, and kept it by her in a bag of red leather until she died.

AS YOU CAME FROM THE
HOLY LAND

As you came from the holy land
    Of Walsinghame
Met you not with my true love
    By the way as you came?

How shall I know your true love
    That have met many one
As I went to the holy land
    That have come, that have gone?

She is neither white nor brown
    But as the heavens fair,
There is none hath a form so divine
    In the earth or the air.

Such a one did I meet, good sir,
    Such an angelic face,
Who like a queen, like a nymph, did appear
    By her gait, by her grace.

She hath left me here all alone,
    All alone as unknown,
Who sometimes did me lead with herself,
    And me lov'd as her own.

What's the cause that she leaves you alone
    And a new way doth take;
Who loved you once as her own
    And her joy did you make?

I have lov'd her all my youth,
    But now old, as you see,
Love likes not the falling fruit
    From the withered tree.

Know that love is a careless child
    And forgets promise past,
He is blind, he is deaf when he list
    And in faith never fast.

His desire is a dureless content
    And a trustless joy,
He is won with a world of despair
    And is lost with a toy.

Of womenkind such indeed is the love
    Or the word love abused
Under which many childish desires
    And conceits are excus'd.

But true love is a durable fire
    In the mind ever burning;
Never sick, never old, never dead,
    From itself never turning.

FROM THE LIE

Go, soul, the body's guest
    Upon a thankless arrant,
Fear not to touch the best,
    The truth shall be thy warrant:
Go since I needs must die,
    And give the world the lie.

Say to the Court it glows,
    And shines like rotten wood,
Say to the Church it shows
    What's good, and doth no good.
If Church and Court reply,
    Then give them both the lie.

Tell potentates they live
    Acting by others' action,
Not loved unless they give,
    Not strong but by affection.
If potentates reply,
    Give potentates the lie.

Tell men of high condition,
    That manage the estate,
Their purpose is ambition,
    Their practice only hate:
And if they once reply,
    Then give them all the lie. . . .

Tell faith it's fled the city,
    Tell how the country erreth,
Tell manhood shakes off pity,
    Tell virtue least preferreth
And if they do reply,
    Spare not to give the lie.

So when thou hast as I
    Commanded thee, done blabbing,
Although to give the lie
    Deserves no less than stabbing,
Stab at thee he that will,
    No stab thy soul can kill.

EVEN SUCH IS TIME

Even such is Time, which takes in trust
Our youth, our joys, our all we have,
And pays us but with earth and dust:
Who in the dark and silent grave,
When we have wandered all our ways,
Shuts up the story of our days.
But from this earth, this grave, this dust,
My God shall raise me up, I trust.

John Donne at the age of eighteen

THREE

John Donne
(*1573-1631*)

John Donne: Anne Donne: Undone. Good poets make bad
puns, and that most wry play on his own name and his wife's
name was forced out of John Donne—who is pronounced
dunne—after the two of them had married in secret, without
the consent of his young wife's powerful, rich, ambitious father.

This marriage in 1602 landed Anne (who was seventeen) in
despair, and Donne (who was twenty-nine) in prison, and in
poverty too, since Anne's father had persuaded the Lord
Chancellor of England to dismiss his unwanted son-in-law from
a high enviable post as the Chancellor's secretary. After that
he had tried (but had failed) to get the Archbishop to de-
clare the marriage between John and Anne Donne unlawful
and void.

Great politicians, all men with great power, like those who
serve them to do as they are told; they like them to conform,
and to avoid being rash. But the trouble with poets is that
they may have a great power of their own, which will not
take orders from other people. They may have "hearts," as we
say, the heart responds to impulses, and gives orders. It says
"do this," "do that," "write a poem," "go off with that girl";

and it is done straight away, to the poet's undoing—*John Donne: Anne Donne: Undone.*

As readers we are lucky, we inherit the poems. The poet, like Donne, often has to suffer the consequence.

Think, then, of this poet in London in 1594, when he was twenty-one, the fieriest, the most impetuous, the most intelligent, the most inquisitive, the most energetic, the most riddling, and most attractive of all Elizabethans of his age: he was tall, very straight, and moved very gracefully. He was independent and well-to-do (Donne's father, who had died when he was three, had been a rich ironmonger in the City). He knew everything, after Oxford and studying law in Lincoln's Inn and traveling abroad, and he seemed very up to the minute, a whole *avant-garde* in himself. Also he was a little peculiar in a different way, since he was a Catholic when every ordinary young Londoner was an ardent Protestant. His younger brother had just died in prison, which he had earned by hiding a Catholic priest in his lodgings.

When this panther of a young man was not in a black, absent, lonely mood, words came out of him in company full of delight, sparkle, and surprise. What was more important, though he might talk outrageously, was John Donne's face: he had the grave extraordinary look about him which newly-created Adam might have had as the first man, everything seeming to him strange and young. He easily blushed, or went pale. People were fascinated by him, women especially, whether girls or mothers or grandmothers.

Anne More, daughter of Sir George More, Lieutenant of the Tower of London, was not the first girl he was in love with. Before they met in the Lord Chancellor's house in the Strand, where Anne was living with her aunt—before their "first strange and fatal interview," and "all desires which thereof did ensue"—love affairs had made him write love poems more open and passionate than any others in English.

Who the girls were is unknown. But no one can forget the lines which Donne wrote about them—"Some that have deeper digg'd Love's mine than I," "But now I have drunk thy sweet salt tears," "I taught my silks their whistling to forbear," "When, by thy scorn, O murdress, I am dead," or

> I long to talk with some old lover's ghost
> Who died before the god of Love was born.

Donne interrupted love affairs, or escaped from them, by travel in Spain and Italy (so his money vanished), and by joining naval expeditions to Cadiz and out into the Atlantic by the Azores.

Everything he felt deep enough inside him, or everything which intrigued him enough, produced poems, compact with all the special particulars that caught his eye, his ear, his sense of touch, or his sense of smell. Buds on trees, rough bark on elm branches, the Thames overflowing, primroses, flowers washed away on a flood, the peak of Teneriffe emerging from haze very high over the Atlantic, the wind roaring through the ruins of an abbey, a new word he picked up and liked, such as "hydroptic," a print in a book of a whale or a mermaid, meridians and parallels on a chart or a map— every such item might come out in a poem, and might suggest some curious parallel idea.

Before going to sea, he said in a poem to the girl he was leaving, or rather in a poem about her tears:

> Weep me not dead, in thine arms, but forbear
> To teach the sea, what it may do too soon.

He gave her a miniature of himself, as somebody now would give a snapshot, because he might die, or if he came back, might not look the fair and delicate lover she had known;

his hands might be rough and brown, his face and chest might be hairy,

> My body a sack of bones, broken within,
> And powder's blue stains scatter'd on my skin.

On board ship he wrote a poem describing a storm, how waves had been driven forward "like a rolling trench," how the tackling snapped "like too-high-stretched treble strings,"

> And from our tatter'd sails, rags drop down so
> As from one hang'd in chains a year ago.

Then he wrote a second poem about the calm which followed near the Azores, and the heat, how everyone on board seemed to walk in a hot oven, and lay on the hatches like sacrifices on altars, how

> If in despite of these, we swim, that hath
> No more refreshing than our brimstone bath,
> But from the sea into the ship we turn
> Like parboil'd wretches, on the coals to burn.

When travel and high living had reduced the money Donne inherited, his need—and his ambition—took him into a new life, right into the depth of government as the Lord Chancellor's trusted, very able, very much admired secretary.

But there he had met Anne More, and calculation and caution and ambition had given way to a heart which did not understand the word "No," and to that impulsive secret marriage in 1602, which meant prison (not for long), and being humble, though he hated crawling and humility, toward Anne's father and the Lord Chancellor; and which also led to year after year of poverty and insecurity, in which he and Anne had more and more children to feed.

In the end John Donne became a clergyman. He did not much want to, but he had long ago ceased to be a Catholic, and no one, however many years he waited, was going to give him the kind of post he had enjoyed under the Chancellor. It was the King (James I) who declared that Mr. Donne would be a good preacher, and ought to be ordained, which would be a way out of his troubles. Once he made up his mind Donne gave all the force of his heart and his intellect to being the new solemn Doctor of Divinity who now preached before the King as a royal chaplain.

Two years later Anne died, in 1617, leaving him with seven young children. She was only thirty-three.

Poetry flooded back into him. Years before, when he was rejected by one of the girls he loved before his secret marriage to Anne, he had discovered an important thing about grief and love and loss and poems—that making poems, making shapes of words out of a grief which tears you to bits, can help to keep you alive, and make the grief possible to bear.

> I thought, if I could draw my pains
> Through rhyme's vexation I should them allay,
> Grief brought to numbers cannot be so fierce,
> For, he tames it, that fetters it in verse.

Grief had him again. But he was now forty-four, he was middle-aged, not young. When a poet is young, he can love, absolutely, without any caution, without any interference. Life and position and responsibilities have not crowded in on him. When he is old, or older, a poet who believes in God may find that he is free only, or that he wants only, to be passionate about God. Once love for a girl explained everything. Now perhaps things can be explained only by loving God, or talking with him in poems.

Since it was now *John Donne: Anne Donne: Undone* a second time, since Anne was dead,

> Since she, whom I lov'd, hath paid her last debt

> To Nature, and to hers and my good is dead,
> And her soul early into heav'n is ravished

—since this is my condition, said Donne,

> Wholly on heavenly things my mind is set.

And in that way the grave Dr. Donne became a love poet a second time, and wrote poems even more flaming and strong. He wrote lines, again, in these poems to God, which I think— or hope—you may never forget once you have taken them in.

Here are some of them: "One short sleep past, we wake eternally," "Churches are best for prayer, that have least light," "Oh my black soul! now thou art summonèd," "Burn off my rusts and my deformity," "Batter my heart, three person'd God,"

> At the round earth's imagined corners, blow
> Your trumpets, angels.

He preached sermons in which the bell tolls, as splendid and dark as his poems. He was made Dean of St. Paul's Cathedral, and lived, after Anne's death, another thirteen years of much holiness and repentance. Then, when he felt his own death coming, he posed for an artist in his study, with braziers of charcoal glowing around him, naked inside his winding sheet, "with his eyes shut, and with so much sheet turned aside as might show his lean, pale, and deathlike face."

He kept the portrait by his bed where he could see it, till he died (on March 31, 1631). A statue was then carved from it in white marble, and placed in his cathedral of St. Paul's.

The statue was only a little scorched in the Great Fire of London thirty-five years later, and you can see it still in the rebuilt St. Paul's, as intriguing and sharp as an image in Donne's poems. He had ordered a statue of Anne from the same sculptor, Nicholas Stone, and had placed it above her grave in another city church, St. Clement Danes. But unfortunately this disappeared a long while ago.

Exactly eight days before he died, Donne wrote a last poem as fresh as any he had ever written when he was in love with girls, and not with death, the poem (page 40) which begins:

Since I am coming to that holy room
    Where with thy choir of saints for evermore
I shall be made thy music.

Such was the death of a poet who walked through London filled with a violence of heart and a pride which could be free only in loving when he was young, in his God when he was old.

THE SUN RISING

Busy old fool, unruly Sun,
Why dost thou thus,
Through windows, and through curtains call on us?
Must to thy motions lovers' seasons run?
Saucy pedantic wretch, go chide
Late school-boys, and sour prentices,
Go tell court-huntsmen, that the King will ride,
Call country ants to harvest offices;
Love, all alike, no season knows, nor clime,
Nor hours, days, months, which are the rags of time.

Thy beams, so reverend, and strong
Why shouldst thou think?
I could eclipse and cloud them with a wink,
But that I would not lose her sight so long:
If her eyes have not blinded thine,
Look, and to-morrow late, tell me,
Whether both th' Indias of spice and mine
Be where thou left'st them, or lie here with me.
Ask for those kings whom thou saw'st yesterday,
And thou shalt hear, All here in one bed lay.

She is all states, and all princes, I,
Nothing else is.
Princes do but play us; compar'd to this,
All honour's mimic; all wealth alchimy.
Thou Sun art half as happy as we,
In that the world's contracted thus;
Thine age asks ease, and since thy duties be

To warm the world, that's done in warming us.
Shine here to us, and thou art every where;
This bed thy centre is, these walls, thy sphere.

FROM THE ANNIVERSARY

All kings, and all their favourites,
    All glory of honours, beauties, wits,
The sun itself, which makes times, as they pass,
Is elder by a year, now, than it was
When thou and I first one another saw:
All other things to their destruction draw,
    Only our love hath no decay;
This, no to-morrow hath, nor yesterday,
Running it never runs from us away,
But truly keeps his first, last, everlasting day. . . .

FROM ELEGY XVI, ON HIS MISTRESS

By our first strange and fatal interview,
By all desires which thereof did ensue,
By our long starving hopes, by that remorse
Which my words' masculine persuasive force
Begot in thee, and by the memory
Of hurts, which spies and rivals threatened me,
I calmly beg: But by thy father's wrath,
By all pains, which want and divorcement hath,
I conjure thee, and all the oaths which I
And thou have sworn to seal joint constancy,
Here I unswear, and overswear them thus,
Thou shalt not love by ways so dangerous.
Temper, O fair Love, love's impetuous rage,
Be my true mistress still, not my feign'd page;
I'll go, and, by thy kind leave, leave behind
Thee, only worthy to nurse in my mind,
Thirst to come back; O if thou die before,
My soul from other lands to thee shall soar.
Thy (else almighty) beauty cannot move
Rage from the seas, nor thy love teach them love,
Nor tame wild Boreas' harshness; thou hast read
How roughly he in pieces shivered
Fair Orithea, whom he swore he lov'd.
Fall ill or good, 'tis madness to have prov'd
Dangers unurg'd; feed on this flattery,
That absent lovers one in th'other be.
Dissemble nothing, not a boy, nor change
Thy body's habit, nor mind's; be not strange
To thy self only; all will spy in thy face

A blushing womanly discovering grace. . . .
When I am gone, dream me some happiness,
Nor let thy looks our long hid love confess,
Nor praise, nor dispraise me, nor bless nor curse
Openly love's force, nor in bed fright thy nurse
With midnight's startings, crying out, oh, oh
Nurse, O my love is slain, I saw him go
O'er the white Alps alone; I saw him, I,
Assail'd, fight, taken, stabb'd, bleed, fall, and die.
Augur me better chance, except dread Jove
Think it enough for me to have had thy love.

DEATH, BE NOT PROUD

Death, be not proud, though some have callèd thee
Mighty and dreadful, for thou art not so,
For those, whom thou think'st thou dost overthrow,
Die not, poor Death; nor yet canst thou kill me.
From rest and sleep, which but thy picture be,
Much pleasure, then from thee, much more must flow,
And soonest our best men with thee do go,
Rest of their bones, and soul's delivery.
Thou art slave to fate, chance, kings, and desperate men,
And dost with poison, war, and sickness dwell,
And poppy or charms can make us sleep as well,
And better than thy stroke; why swell'st thou then?
One short sleep past, we wake eternally,
And Death shall be no more; Death, thou shalt die.

HYMN TO GOD MY GOD, IN MY SICKNESS

Since I am coming to that holy room,
 Where, with thy choir of saints for evermore,
I shall be made thy music; as I come
 I tune the instrument here at the door,
 And what I must do then, think here before.

Whilst my physicians by their love are grown
 Cosmographers, and I their map, who lie
Flat on this bed, that by them may be shown
 That this is my south-west discovery,
*Per fretum febris,** by these straits to die,

I joy, that in these straits, I see my west;
 For, though their currents yield return to none,
What shall my west hurt me? As west and east
 In all flat maps (and I am one) are one,
 So death doth touch the Resurrection.

Is the Pacific Sea my home? Or are
 The Eastern riches? Is Jerusalem?
Anyan, and Magellan, and Gibraltar,
 All straits, and none but straits, are ways to them,
 Whether where Japhet dwelt, or Cham, or Sem.

* By the strait of fever.

40

We think that Paradise and Calvary,
 Christ's Cross, and Adam's tree, stood in one place;
Look, Lord, and find both Adams met in me;
 As the first Adam's sweat surrounds my face,
 May the last Adam's blood my soul embrace.

So, in his purple wrapp'd, receive me, Lord,
 By these his thorns give me his other crown;
And as to others' souls I preach'd thy word,
 Be this my text, my sermon to mine own,
 Therefore that he may raise the Lord throws down.

John Milton   *From the painting in the National Portrait Gallery*

FOUR

John Milton
(*1608-1674*)

I think we might have disliked John Milton if we had met him, or might have felt small—dislike often comes from feeling small in somebody's presence—when he was about. He was not a very large or masculine-seeming man; he looked, at any rate when he was young, slight, and very fair, and elegant.

When he was a student at Cambridge, other students, rather to his annoyance, called him Domina or the Lady—"The Lady of Christ's College." They probably felt his superiority, and were getting their own back.

The elegant and feminine young man had a very good brain. He was quick, very learned already. Since he was twelve, his father had encouraged him to sit up reading in their London home until after midnight. He wrote poems in English and in Latin. He could write a letter as well in Greek as Latin, could read French, Italian, and Hebrew; and he was impatient perhaps of other people of his own age who were not so much in earnest already about life and time, and, before long, about politics and such large matters as truth and liberty.

We might very likely have resented his ambition, the way he was sure of himself, and determined to compete against the greatest poets of all the past centuries, and leave behind, if he could, something which could be read in future centuries.

Later, when he married a girl from a country manor house where she was used to fun and games, and brought her to London, his serious way of living seemed to her rather dull; and she would hear cries coming upstairs from her learned husband's two nephews, one of them ten, the other nine. Milton was beating their Latin into them (he did it with so much effect that they could read any page of Latin at sight within a year). Mrs. Milton left, and went home to her mother, and didn't come back for several years.

But then she and her family were Cavaliers, on the side of King Charles, and her husband was a Puritan, on the side of liberty and republics.

A Puritan, yes, but a very peculiar one, who made his own decisions, and had become more and more alive, since childhood, to all the best of delights.

John Milton's father was a "scrivener": a man who drew up law documents and acted for people in their business affairs. But when he wasn't scratching a quill pen squeakily over the page, he composed songs for the lute (generally religious ones). He taught his son to play the lute, and the viol, and the organ, and to sing; and Milton in turn made his nephews sing, in between the severities of their teaching. He would sing very cheerfully himself when he suffered the throbbing pains of gout in his blind old age.

Music was one of Milton's delights. He liked rivers and shining water, especially the Thames—he looked on the Thames as his own special river. He liked valleys and plains, on either side of a river between hills; also villages with thick elm trees, which hid or revealed, as he walked past them, the sparkling of stars at night. He liked the way bushes grow like tufts, rounded and solid, out of hillsides. Also the very quiet grayness which came across the elmy riverside fields near London at daybreak—he was always up very early—or in the evening. In the summer, he liked wide hazy skies swelling with white thunderclouds—"hills of snow and lofts of pilèd thunder"; in the autumn, fallen leaves floating on streams. Scents on the air, scents of spring or rain or roses, pleased him—or the smell of spices from the East (which perhaps came to him out of warehouses in London).

As much as anything he was delighted by the spangle of stars—especially the Morning Star or Evening Star by itself in the eastern sky or the western sky, or by the glow of the moon in a wide sky, in between clouds or through clouds, and the glitter of its light on the wet grass between shadows.

> The hornèd moon to shine by night
> Amongst her spangled sisters bright

are lines he wrote when he was fifteen. He enjoyed poetry ancient and modern about sights and sounds of the country and country activities. Liking ships, and the thought of them pushing through strange seas past Ophir or near Arabia, where the spices blew out from the shore, he enjoyed atlases and the captivating names of places such as Mozambique, or the isles of Ternate and Tidore, or "Mombaza, and Quiloa and Melind." The people who walked in his mind included ambassadors

> From India and the golden Chersoness
> And utmost Indian Isle Taprobane,
> Dusk faces with white silk'n turbants wreath'd.

Everything of this kind which Milton liked he thought of almost as though it came out of a huge colored box of crystallized fruits, agreeable to "nature's part" in him. He wasn't against this nature's part, but being a Puritan, he believed we each have a power to distinguish right and wrong; he was for liberty; he was against tyrants and kings, and his "nature's

part" and his power to make poems had to be devoted to all
these greater and grander purposes.

When the Civil War broke out between King and Parliament, or as Milton saw it, between tyrant and people, poems
did not seem the kind of writing which would work on his fellow Englishmen quickly enough. So "in the cool element of
prose," as he called it, Milton told England in pamphlets
about Truth, who "never comes into the world but like a
bastard, to the ignominy of him who brought her forth," and
Conscience, and Liberty, and freedom to think and write,
and that kings—since he preferred "Queen Truth to King
Charles"—were not above right and wrong and were answera-
ble for tyranny.

After the King was beheaded, Milton was given a high office in the government under Cromwell—the Secretaryship of
the Foreign Tongues. One of his duties was to write, in sono-
rous, perfect Latin, the letters of state from the government
of England to foreign governments. For instance, he had to
write letter after letter of official indignation when the Wal-
densians on Vaudois, Protestants in remote Alpine valleys
above Turin, were terribly massacred in 1655 by a Catholic army. In between these letters Milton wrote his sonnet (page
51) about the bones of these poor Vaudois lying "on the
Alpine mountains cold," and the rolling of their women and
children down the rocks.

By that time Milton had been blind for several years. He
had inherited weak sight from his mother. Staying up late to
read as a child had given him headaches and bothered his
eyes. Reading for his learned, very long pamphlets troubled
his eyes again, and he passed slowly into a dark world.

About two years before King Charles II came back, blind
Milton started the great poem he always wanted to write and
leave behind him, in which he would use all his ability to
build lines, for pages on end, out of a strong sweetness of

sound, all nature's part in him, all the things which had given him delight, to explain God and Man, Satan and Knowledge, and the Expulsion of our First Parents from Paradise their happy seat into a world of sorrow and labor. Then Charles was restored, Milton went into hiding in London, likely to be condemned to death for the words he had written against tyranny and the executed King.

But he was pardoned—though some of his pamphlets against oppression and royalty were ordered to be seized and burned by the common hangman—and he went on composing his *Paradise Lost*.

He had always made up his poems very early in the day after waking up, sometimes in bed. Much of huge *Paradise Lost* came to him that way. Then with the morning's lines in his head he would wait until a friend or pupil arrived, to take them down. "I want to be milked," blind Milton used to say as he waited.

When he had dictated the last lines (page 57) and when *Paradise Lost* was published at last in 1667, the publisher paid him five pounds for the first edition. In a new-fashioned world of courtiers, it looked an old-fashioned poem. But it has been read ever since, and it made Milton feel that he had done his duty by his gifts.

Milton believed he had sacrificed his eyes to write about liberty. The royalists said his blindness was a just reward for the pamphlets he had written against the dead king. After the Restoration when he was old and poor in his blindness, lucky to be alive, and still busy on *Paradise Lost,* the new king's brother, the Duke of York (who was to be James II), felt curious about this blind old fellow from the time without a king, and went to see him. They talked for a bit. Then the Duke asked him, so the story goes, if his blindness wasn't a judgment for what he had written against Charles I?

"If your Highness thinks that the calamities which befall

us here," Milton replied, "are indications of the wrath of Heaven, in what manner are we to account for the fate of the King your father? The displeasure of Heaven must, upon this supposition, have been much greater against him than against me; for I have only lost my eyes, but he lost his head."

Honors to the poet.

PSALM VIII

O Jehovah our Lord how wondrous great
    And glorious is thy name through all the earth!
So as above the Heavens thy praise to set
    Out of the tender mouths of latest birth,

Out of the mouths of babes and sucklings thou
    Hast founded strength because of all thy foes
To stint th' enemy, and slack th' avenger's brow
    That bends his rage thy providence to oppose.

When I behold thy Heavens, thy fingers' art,
    The moon and stars which thou so bright hast set,
In the pure firmament, then saith my heart,
    O what is man that thou remembrest yet,

And think'st upon him; or of man begot
    That him thou visit'st and of him art found;
Scarce to be less than gods, thou mad'st his lot,
    With honour and with state thou hast him crown'd.

O'er the works of thy hand thou mad'st him lord,
    Thou hast put all under his lordly feet,
All flocks, and herds, by thy commanding word,
    All beasts that in the field or forest meet,

Fowl of the heavens, and fish that through the wet
    Sea-paths in shoals do slide, and know no dearth.
O Jehovah our Lord how wondrous great
    And glorious is thy name through all the earth.

ON HIS DEAD WIFE

Methought I saw my late espoused saint
    Brought to me like Alcestis from the grave,
    Whom Jove's great son to her glad husband gave,
    Rescued from death by force though pale and faint.
Mine as whom washt from spot of child-bed taint,
    Purification in the old Law did save,
    And such, as yet once more I trust to have
    Full sight of her in Heaven without restraint,
Came vested all in white, pure as her mind:
    Her face was veil'd, yet to my fancied sight
    Love, sweetness, goodness, in her person shin'd
So clear, as in no face with more delight.
    But O as to embrace me she enclin'd,
    I waked, she fled, and day brought back my night.

ON THE LATE MASSACRE IN PIEDMONT

Avenge O Lord thy slaughter'd saints, whose bones
    Lie scatter'd on the Alpine mountains cold,
    Ev'n them who kept thy truth so pure of old
    When all our fathers worship't stocks and stones,
Forget not: in thy book record their groans
    Who were thy sheep, and in their ancient fold
    Slain by the bloody Piemontese that roll'd
    Mother with infant down the rocks. Their moans
The vales redoubl'd to the hills, and they
    To Heav'n. Their martyr'd blood and ashes sow
    O'er all th' Italian fields where still doth sway
The triple Tyrant: that from these may grow
    A hundred-fold, who having learnt thy way
    Early may fly the Babylonian woe.

AT A SOLEMN MUSICK

Blest pair of Sirens, pledges of Heav'n's joy,
Sphere-born harmonious sisters, Voice, and Verse,
Wed your divine sounds, and mixt power employ
Dead things with inbreath'd sense able to pierce,
And to our high-rais'd fantasy present,
That undisturbed song of pure consent,
Ay sung before the sapphire-colour'd throne
To him that sits thereon
With saintly shout, and solemn jubilee,
Where the bright Seraphim in burning row
Their loud uplifted angel trumpets blow,
And the Cherubic host in thousand choirs
Touch their immortal harps of golden wires,
With those just Spirits that wear victorious palms,
Hymns devout and holy psalms
Singing everlastingly;
That we on earth with undiscording voice
May rightly answer that melodious noise;
As once we did, till disproportion'd sin
Jarr'd against nature's chime, and with harsh din
Broke the fair musick that all creatures made
To their great Lord, whose love their motion sway'd
In perfect diapason, whilst they stood
In first obedience, and their state of good.
O may we soon again renew that song,
And keep in tune with Heav'n, till God ere long
To his celestial consort us unite,
To live with him, and sing in endless morn of light.

NOW CAME STILL EVENING ON

. . . Now came still Evening on, and Twilight gray
Had in her sober livery all things clad;
Silence accompanied, for beast and bird,
They to their grassy couch, these to their nests
Were slunk, all but the wakeful nightingale;
She all night long her amorous descant sung;
Silence was pleas'd: now glow'd the firmament
With living sapphires: Hesperus that led
The starry host, rode brightest, till the Moon
Rising in clouded majesty, at length
Apparent queen unveil'd her peerless light,
And o'er the dark her silver mantle threw . . . .

JOHN MILTON

EVE TO ADAM

. . . With thee conversing I forget all time,
All seasons and their change, all please alike.
Sweet is the breath of Morn, her rising sweet,
With charm of earliest birds; pleasant the Sun
When first on this delightful land he spreads
His orient beams, on herb, tree, fruit, and flower,
Glistring with dew; fragrant the fertile earth
After soft showers; and sweet the coming on
Of grateful Evening mild, then silent Night
With this her solemn bird and this fair Moon,
And these the Gems of Heav'n, her starry train:
But neither breath of Morn when she ascends
With charm of earliest birds, nor rising Sun
On this delightful land, nor herb, fruit, flower,
Glistring with dew, nor fragrance after showers,
Nor grateful Evening mild, nor silent Night
With this her solemn bird, nor walk by Moon,
Or glittering starlight without thee is sweet . . . .

AFTER THE DEATH OF SAMSON

. . . Come, come, no time for lamentation now,
Nor much more cause, Samson hath quit himself
Like Samson, and heroicly hath finish'd
A life heroic, on his enemies
Fully reveng'd, hath left them years of mourning,
And lamentation to the Sons of Caphtor
Through all Philistian bounds. To Israel
Honour hath left, and freedom, let but them
Find courage to lay hold on this occasion,
To himself and father's house eternal fame;
And which is best and happiest yet, all this
With God not parted from him, as was fear'd,
But favouring and assisting to the end.
Nothing is here for tears, nothing to wail
Or knock the breast, no weakness, no contempt,
Dispraise, or blame, nothing but well and fair,
And what may quiet us in a death so noble.
Let us go find the body . . . .

Chorus

> All is best, though we oft doubt,
> What th' unsearchable dispose
> Of highest wisdom brings about,
> And ever best found in the close.
> Oft he seems to hide his face,
> But unexpectedly returns
> And to his faithful Champion hath in place
> Bore witness gloriously; whence Gaza mourns

And all that band them to resist
His uncontrollable intent;
His servants he with new acquist
Of true experience from this great event
With peace and consolation hath dismist,
And calm of mind all passion spent.

ADAM AND EVE ARE EXPELLED
FROM PARADISE
(The last lines of *Paradise Lost*)

. . . So spake our Mother Eve, and Adam heard
Well pleas'd, but answer'd not; for now too nigh
Th' Arch-Angel stood, and from the other hill
To their fixt station, all in bright array
The Cherubim descended; on the ground
Gliding meteorous, as ev'ning mist
Ris'n from a river o'er the marish glides,
And gathers ground fast at the labourer's heel
Homeward returning. High in front advanc't,
The brandisht sword of God before them blaz'd
Fierce as a comet; which with torrid heat,
And vapour as the Libyan air adust,
Began to parch that temperate clime; whereat
In either hand the hastning Angel caught
Our lingring Parents, and to th' Eastern Gate
Led them direct, and down the cliff as fast
To the subjected plain; then disappear'd.
They looking back, all th' eastern side beheld
Of Paradise, so late their happy seat,
Wav'd over by that flaming brand, the gate
With dreadful faces throng'd and fiery arms:
Some natural tears they dropp'd, but wip'd them soon;
The World was all before them, where to choose
Their place of rest, and providence their guide:
They hand in hand with wandring steps and slow,
Through Eden took their solitary way.

Henry Vaughan's tombstone, Llansantffraed churchyard

FIVE

Henry Vaughan, Silurist
(1621-1695)

Henry Vaughan was a poet who liked sparkle and running water and skies when they were very clear and rinsed with light; and also when they were dark and full of stars. Early morning was one of his favorite times, when no one else was about, when the light across the Welsh valley he lived in, over the river, over the hills, over the small mountains, seemed to unite this world, in which men die, to another world of very pure eternity or everlastingness. Our own world in these morning lights seemed to him to be transformed by a glory from elsewhere.

For nearly all his life Henry Vaughan lived in a small crowded house, with a small farm attached, on the side of a hill in Breconshire. Below the house ran the highway to London, below the highway was the River Usk (he was called the Swan of Usk), which he loved and thought of as a being with its own personality. Across the Usk the sky rested on the Black Mountains, not very high, but decidedly a wall of this world, sometimes black after sunset, sometimes golden when the sun rose, sometimes very blue, or violet. Behind the house where the Vaughans lived, called Trenewydd in Welsh, and Newton in English, behind the hill called the Allt, the sky and the light were reflected in a wide shallow lake surrounded with church towers.

When a mist trailed over this "drowsy lake" of Llangorse (nowadays much used by sailing dinghies with colored sails), Vaughan believed that he was seeing the birth of clouds.

Not very much is known about Vaughan. He was never famous. No one bothered much about his few books. He had been dead more than a hundred years before other poets rediscovered him and realized that he had written great poems. No one troubled to draw him or paint him, so in place of a portrait I have put his gravestone from the churchyard of Llansantffraed, not far from Vaughan's house, the Latin of which says that the inscription was the one he asked to have on his tomb:

Unprofitable servant:
Greatest of sinners
Here I lie
Glory   Have Mercy

Vaughan, you will see from the gravestone, is called *Henricus Vaughan. Siluris. M.D.*—M.D., doctor of medicine, because he was the local doctor, Siluris because he was Welsh, and proud of it: Henry Vaughan the Silurist, one of the Silures, which was the name by which the Romans had known the great tribe of the people of South Wales.

Henry was one of twins. He and his twin brother Thomas were born at Newton in 1621. Welsh was their first language. But if you were a Welshman you got on best in the world by knowing English; and these two clever twins, "the bright Gemini," a friend called them afterward, would have been taught in English by the schoolmaster they were sent to, a clergyman a few miles away across the Usk.

When they were seventeen their father, who was a Justice of the Peace in Breconshire, sent the twins to Oxford. Thomas was going to be a parson (though the mysteries of alchemy and science were the things he most liked), and he continued at the university. Henry was to be a lawyer, and went on to London. There he mixed for a time with poets, older and younger. The Civil War broke out in 1642, and Henry Vaughan, now twenty-one, was called home by his father.

All the world seemed breaking up. Friends turned to enemies, families divided between King and Parliament. Oxen dragged cannon about the lanes of Wales and England. Blood soaked into the fields. It seems that (for a while) the twin brothers served in the King's army, Thomas (not yet a parson) as captain, Henry as lieutenant, in the same troop of Welshmen. Henry saw friends killed beside him, then when the Civil War slackened and halted he went back to his rather humble job as law clerk to a Welsh judge.

But for the war, he perhaps felt, he might have done great things in London. Still, he was at home again in his vale. He had fallen in love and married, he was back in the small eight-room house opposite the mountains, with his parents, his sister, his younger brother. And his twin Thomas, now a parson, was back, too, and was rector of their parish church, down the London highway at Llansantffraed. The bright Gemini were still in their twenties.

Then something happened to change Vaughan from being a poet who had only written occasional, pretty, rather ordinary poems. Darkness came round the house. The twins very much loved their younger brother William: it seems that he too had been in the Civil War, had been wounded, invalided home, and had there, at Newton, died of his wounds, in 1648—a death, at home, in the valley, in the family, where, war or no war, everything had seemed genial and everlasting. And one of Henry's young children may have died as well.

So Henry Vaughan thought about death and life and love and childhood, and a world of light, like the light over the

Breconshire mountains and the valley in the mornings, in which those one loved continued as spirits beyond death.

I imagine him doing three things, at times mooning around broken and lost with grief, at times shrugging his shoulders and going to drink defiantly with his twin, at the rectory; at times having long attacks of remorse.

Then, for consolation, he must have read the poems in which an older poet, George Herbert, wrote down, in the clearest and most subtle everyday English, his arguments with God and his comfort in accepting a divine will and authority.

At any rate, he now started writing poems again, at first rather like Herbert's, then poems very much his own, full of sparkle and light and remembered ecstasy, and praise of that eternity in which the dead went on living; and I imagine him now tiptoeing through the bedrooms (which in those days usually opened from one to another), past the closed curtains of their four-poster beds, past others asleep on the floor of the hall or main living room, before sunrise; and then thinking, as the air became wonderful, as he took in the blending of earth and heaven, as he smelled the scent of what he called "the now primros'd fields," how such a sparkle and clearness of everything resembled the years before the war, in which the three brothers had lived an innocent, entirely unthreatened, entirely happy childhood. Or he might go out at night in the same way, under the moon or under the stars. He would come back making a poem, settling his unhappiness that way, feeling that his brother and his child had been absorbed again into such an innocence.

I think he may have written the great poem which begins:

> I saw Eternity the other night
> Like a great ring of pure and endless light
>   All calm, as it was bright,
> And round beneath it, Time in hours, days, years,

> Driv'n by the spheres
> Like a vast shadow mov'd, in which the world
> And all her train were hurl'd,

after seeing over Newton, and the Usk, and the hills, one of those huge rings of light which often surround the moon.

Anyhow, the poems were written, then published, two years after William's death, in a book which Vaughan called *Silex Scintillans,* the Sparkling Flint, since he thought of his heart as a flint from the hardness of which tears had been pressed. By dying, he said, he had lived again.

Soon he had more trouble. His wife died. The Parliament turned his twin out of the rectory at Llansantffraed, saying that he drank, and swore, and did not preach, and had fought against the Parliament, and the twin went off to Oxford again and returned to alchemy. Henry Vaughan, now alone, wrote a few more poems. One (page 70) was

> They are all gone into the world of light!

—all of them, his dead young brother, his dead child, his dead young wife.

Then the desire to write, perhaps the ability to write, left him again. Still young, he became a doctor. He was too busy for poems, he never wrote a book he planned about shooting stars, he married again, had more children, inherited the family house (since he had been the eldest of the three sons, the first of the twins to be born), and lived on in his primrosed valley into old age, until he died in 1695 when he was seventy-three, and was buried under the yew tree in the churchyard of the Church of St. Brigit (that is the meaning of Llansantffraed), who was the Celtic saint of light, and spring, and nature.

Scholars have said that Henry Vaughan did one very Welsh thing in his English poems—he often used, and specially loved, the word "white" (*gwyn* in Welsh), which the Welsh use for more than white, for everything which is fair, and clear, and blessed, and happy.

FROM COCK-CROWING

Father of lights! what sunny seed
What glance of day hast thou confin'd
Into this bird? To all the breed
This busy ray thou hast assign'd;
Their magnetism works all night,
And dreams of Paradise and light.

Their eyes watch for the morning hue,
Their little grain expelling night
So shines and sings, as if it knew
The path unto the house of light,
It seems their candle, howe'er done,
Was tinn'd and lighted at the sun. . . .

PEACE

My soul, there is a country
        Far beyond the stars,
Where stands a wingèd sentry
        All skilful in the wars;
There, above noise and danger,
        Sweet peace sits crown'd with smiles,
And one born in a manger
        Commands the beauteous files.
He is thy gracious friend,
        And (O my soul awake!)
Did in pure love descend
        To die here for thy sake.
If thou canst get but thither,
        There grows the flower of peace,
The rose that cannot wither,
        Thy fortress, and thy ease;
Leave then thy foolish ranges;
        For none can thee secure,
But one, who never changes,
        Thy God, thy life, thy cure.

FROM THE RAINBOW

Still young and fine! but what is still in view
We slight as old and soil'd, though fresh and new.
How bright wert thou, when Shem's admiring eye
Thy burnisht, flaming arch did first descry!
When Terah, Nahor, Haran, Abram, Lot,
The youthful world's gray fathers in one knot,
Did with intentive looks watch every hour
For thy new light, and trembled at each shower!
When thou dost shine darkness looks white and fair,
Storms turn to music, clouds to smiles and air:
Rain gently spends his honey-drops, and pours
Balm on the cleft earth, milk on grass and flowers. . . .

FROM LOOKING BACK

Fair, shining mountains of my pilgrimage,
  And flow'ry vales, whose flow'rs were stars:
The days and nights of my first happy age;
  An age without distaste and wars:
When I by thoughts ascend your sunny heads,
  And mind those sacred, midnight lights
By which I walk'd, when curtain'd rooms and beds
  Confin'd, or seal'd up other sights:
        O then how bright
        And quick a light
  Doth brush my heart and scatter night;
        Chasing that shade
        Which my sins made,
  While I so spring, as if I could not fade! . . .

THE SHOWER

Waters above! eternal springs!
The dew, that silvers the dove's wings!
O welcome, welcome to the sad:
Give dry dust drink; drink that makes glad!
Many fair ev'nings, many flow'rs
Sweeten'd with rich and gentle showers
Have I enjoy'd, and down have run
Many a fine and shining sun;
But never till this happy hour
Was blest with such an evening-shower!

FROM THEY ARE ALL GONE INTO THE WORLD OF LIGHT

They are all gone into the world of light!
    And I alone sit ling'ring here;
Their very memory is fair and bright,
    And my sad thoughts doth clear.

It glows and glitters in my cloudy breast
    Like stars upon some gloomy grove,
Or those faint beams in which this hill is drest,
    After the sun's remove.

I see them walking in an air of glory,
    Whose light doth trample on my days:
My days, which are at best but dull and hoary,
    Mere glimmering and decays.

O holy hope! and high humility.
    High as the heavens above!
These are your walks, and you have shew'd them me
    To kindle my cold love.

Dear, beauteous death! the jewel of the just,
    Shining nowhere, but in the dark,
What mysteries do lie beyond thy dust,
    Could man outlook that mark!

He that hath found some fledg'd bird's nest, may know
 At first sight, if the bird be flown;
But what fair well or grove he sings in now,
 That is to him unknown.

And yet, as angels in some brighter dreams
 Call to the soul, when man doth sleep:
So some strange thoughts transcend our wonted themes,
 And into glory peep. . . .

John Dryden   *From the painting in the National Portrait Gallery*

SIX

John Dryden
(*1631-1700*)

Poems used to be spoken of as though they were flowers, our word "anthology" (from the Greek) meaning a choice or picking of flowers.

Don't be too ready to think this stupid or sentimental. It may seem out of date, but if you think about it, flowers are young, and poems are young, if they are good ones; they stay young and fresh: as they were when they were first made.

The poet who made them, as a rule, also stays in our minds either young or without any particular age. He *is* his poems, but it often happens in fact that poets do write some of their best poems when they are as young as eighteen or twenty or twenty-five.

John Milton was no more than an undergraduate at Cambride when he wrote in his "Ode on the Morning of Christ's Nativity," which we have never ceased to read:

> See how from far upon the eastern road
> The star-led wizards haste with odours sweet.

Blake was writing poems, good poems too, when he was twelve. Coleridge was twenty-four when he started writing out his vision of "Kubla Khan" and was interrupted by the "person from Porlock." By the same age Keats had written his poem to a nightingale and his poem about the "Season of mists and mellow fruitfulness" (add another year, and Keats, at twenty-five, was dead and buried in his Roman graveyard). In France there was Arthur Rimbaud, who had written, not just a poem or two, but all his poems, in four years, by the time he was nineteen, and had given up poetry for good, or for business.

John Dryden is altogether different. His poems (and Dryden himself) seem to have been born halfway between young and not young.

A rather feeble poet wrote about him:

> Great Dryden did not early great appear,
> Faintly distinguish'd in his thirtieth year.

Comically put, but true; and I do not find it easy to imagine Dryden much before he was twenty-nine or thirty—to imagine him when he was a child, or eighteen, or twenty.

Later on, yes. Later on, famous, acknowledged the greatest writer in London, it is easy to see him inside one's mind presiding at Will's Coffee House, in Bow Street, near Covent Garden, cherry-cheeked, urbane, a bit pleased with himself, quite certain that he wrote with more fire than anyone else; rather short, rather plump, and commonly known—by those who did not like him—as Poet Squab, or Squab, or Old Squab ("squab" meaning short and fat, like a squab, which is a plump young featherless pigeon in the nest).

I rather suppose that Dryden always looked mature. For one thing he was the eldest of fourteen children, three brothers, ten sisters, all stuffed into a not very rich manor house in Northamptonshire, at Titchmarsh, among the hay meadows of the River Nene, which winds widely toward the Fen country; and eldest children often have an elderly character.

This first-born child (born in 1631) came of a family of severe Puritans, developed slowly, and was boxed in by troubles and repression—the Civil War, the beheading of the King (this happened just down the road, or down the street, when John Dryden was at school at Westminster), and then the Protectorate. It was said that Dryden's fontanel (the membrane-covered opening in our skulls, with which each of us is born) never closed when he was a baby or in fact until he was twenty-seven; by which time, after Westminster School and Cambridge, John Dryden was a clerk in the office of one of the Cromwellian secretaries of state. John Milton was among his seniors and superiors.

At any rate, he did not sparkle. He may have had a good opinion of himself (his girl cousins in Northamptonshire called him Mr. Conceit), but at an age already when other poets had written themselves into fame, this poet and civil servant had hardly written a line. No one would have pointed to him and said: "That young man is going to be one of the great poets of England." Dryden (who disapproved of saying much that was personal in his prose or poetry) did say of himself at the beginning of his writer's career: "My conversation is slow and dull: my humour saturnine and reserved; in short, I am none of those who endeavor to break jests in company or make repartees." He was to change. But that was Dryden's character to begin with.

Since there were thirteen brothers and sisters to be launched, Dryden could not expect much from his father, who died when he was at Cambridge, and left him only a farm. The rent of this farm allowed him barely enough to exist on. So he had to earn. And when Cromwell died, and the Protectorate ended, and the King over the water came home, and Dryden lost his government clerkship, he began to earn by writing —and not so much at first by writing poems (though he wrote a complimentary poem to see Cromwell into his grave, and another complimentary poem to see Charles II back into his kingdom, and a third one to see the crown on to his head) as by writing plays.

Plays in verse were the way to make money and a reputation.

Under the Protectorate theaters had been closed. They were now reopened. A new crush of courtiers and bright ladies wanted amusing. Dryden wrote them comedies and tragedies, of all kinds. Some of them were bawdy, some not. Some of them were good and successful, some of them were cheap and catchy and also successful, some of them were worthless failures. In 1667, six years after the King's return from exile, and the year after the Fire of London, elderly John Milton had published *Paradise Lost*. Dryden admired it (though it seemed an old-fashioned poem), called on Milton and asked if he might turn it into an opera. Milton gave him leave "to tag his verses" if he wanted to (meaning to put rhymes on the end), and Dryden concocted one of his failures, so very bad it was never performed. He called it *The State of Innocence*. When it was printed, readers found in it verses of the kind which sound good, but are absurd when you trouble to look at them and notice what they really say:

> Seraph and cherub, careless of their charge
> And wanton, in full ease now live at large;
> Unguarded leave the passes of the sky,
> And all dissolved in hallelujahs lie.

A wit observed that he had "heard of anchovies dissolved in sauce, but never of an angel dissolved in hallelujahs."

Yet frequently the verse in Dryden's plays was grand and strong, and the lines often glittered like ore.

After fifteen years of the theater and bringing up his three sons (children of a rather silly, illiterate mother, who was the daughter of an impoverished earl), Dryden, now the King's Poet Laureate, took to poems again, when he was fifty.

The laugh now was always on his side, because there had never been such poems, there had never been satires which destroyed their victims so completely, with such wit, and in such strong, fine, clear English.

When Dryden wrote about one of his chief victims, the (bad) poet and (rather good) playwright Thomas Shadwell, and said:

> The midwife laid her hand on his thick skull,
> With this prophetic blessing—Be thou dull,

Shadwell, who said many nasty and not at all witty or well-expressed things against Dryden, was transformed into a joke forever.

It was as if a giant had picked him up from the street in London and with a laugh had squeezed him between his huge finger and thumb, almost gently, into an eternal absence, into a less than nothing which would always be there to entertain us—also to remind us that all poetry is not about love or moonlight or nightingales or autumn:

> Shadwell alone of all my sons is he
> Who stands confirm'd in full stupidity.
> The rest to some faint meaning make pretence,
> But Shadwell never deviates into sense.

There were three reasons why Dryden wrote that kind of poetry so very well. The poetry he liked best in his younger time had been John Donne's. He soon gave up Donne's odd kinds of intricacy, but Donne had taught him a hard, sharp-edged English with much weight and punch.

That was the first reason. The second was the way the ridiculous or the contemptible fascinated him. At one time—here is a story which may or may not be true—the rather soft character Thomas Otway, another dramatist, lived opposite Dryden, across the street. He called on Dryden at breakfast time, but Dryden's servant said his master had gone to take breakfast with the Earl of Pembroke. Otway told him to say he would come back next morning at the same time. When he crossed the street and climbed the stairs again to Dryden's landing, the servant said Dryden had "just gone to breakfast with the Duke of Buckingham." "The devil he has," Otway exclaimed, and picked up a stick of chalk and wrote in annoyance over Dryden's door:

Here lives Dryden, a poet and a wit,

a wit impling not only a witty talker but also a man who kept fashionable company.

Dryden did not see this till he was up the day after. He quickly told his man to go across the road and ask Otway to breakfast. When Otway arrived, he found that underneath

Here lives Dryden, a poet and a wit,

Dryden had chalked a second line:

This was written by Otway, opposite.

When he had trouble, too, with his publisher, Jacob Tonson, who flattered him (with melons, and gifts of wine), tried to bully him, and cheated him, he acted in much the same way. "Upon trial I find all of your trade are sharpers," he had written to Tonson, "and you not more than others; therefore I have not wholly left you"; and when Tonson sent a message saying no to some small request, Dryden sat down and dashed off the three short, funny, insulting, devastating lines about him which you will find on page 83; he sent the three lines back by the messenger, who was ordered to "Tell the dog that he who wrote these can write more."

But in his satires—here is the third reason why they are so good—Dryden directed his deadly fun, his exactly right words, against people on the opposite side of himself in politics, whom he thought to be stirring up disorder against order.

Dryden wanted order. He was not a rebel: he had lived through enough rebellion, enough trouble ever since he was a boy, enough disorder, enough changes, enough of the Puritans. So he wanted life—and poems as well—to be smooth, social, clear, and strong, and in decent order; and trouble-makers to be cut down to size and shown up.

This "Poet Squab" or "Glorious John" was a conservative. You may—I hope you do—like to think of your poets as anything but that, as rebels, as laws to themselves, as William Blakes or D. H. Lawrences. But with Dryden you just have to accept that conservatism—or a conservative poet, which isn't entirely the same—has sometimes made magnificent poetry, in a situation which has required order and plainest speech.

When Dryden was in London, how pleasant to walk in the afternoon from his house in Gerrard Street to Will's Coffee House in Bow Street, and be the Great Poet of Order, to sit in the best chair on the balcony in the summer, take snuff, and looking out on to Covent Garden, have everyone deferring to him, and young poets asking his advice—because he wrote well in many more kinds of poetry than satire.

This was a correct public life.

At home, or on cheerful summer visits to Northamptonshire (where he liked among other things to go pike fishing in the Nene), he preferred his private life to continue discreetly and cheerfully private.

This was the correct private life to live after a revolution.

Becoming more than ever a squab, more cherry-cheeked, more out of breath, but not out of temper (his words might hit like a fist, but he was very sweet-tempered), Dryden went on writing well to the very end of his life, which came in 1700 (when he was sixty-eight), just after he had overlapped into the new century and had written what was really an epitaph (on page 86) about all those years of war, trouble, eccentricity, untidiness, pestilence, and fire:

> 'Tis well an old age is out
> And time to begin a new.

Oboes and trumpets now played Dryden to his funeral in Westminster Abbey, in the Poet's Corner—though his desire for authority had long changed him from Puritan to Roman Catholic.

Down at Titchmarsh, where he had grown up at the head of that long family, a monument in the church, set there by one of his cousins to commemorate his father and mother, tells the world about Dryden as well: "We boast that he was bred and had his first learning here; where he has often made us happy by his kind visits, and most delightful conversation."

A CHARM

Thou Moon, that aid'st us with thy magic might,
And ye small stars, the scatter'd seeds of light,
Dart your pale beams into this gloomy place,
That the sad powers of the infernal race
May read above what's hid from human eyes,
And in your walks see empires fall and rise.
And ye immortal souls, who once were men,
And now resolv'd to elements again,
Who wait for mortal frames in depths below,
And did before what we are doom'd to do:
Once, twice and thrice, I wave my sacred wand,
Ascend, ascend, ascend at my command.

ZIMRI (THE DUKE OF BUCKINGHAM)

. . . Some of their chiefs were princes of the land;
In the first rank of these did Zimri stand:
A man so various, that he seem'd to be
Not one, but all mankind's epitome.
Stiff in opinions, always in the wrong,
Was every thing by starts, and nothing long:
But in the course of one revolving moon
Was chymist, fiddler, statesman, and buffoon;
Then all for women, painting, rhyming, drinking,
Besides ten thousand freaks that died in thinking.
Blest madman, who could every hour employ
With something new to wish, or to enjoy!
Railing and praising were his usual themes;
And both (to shew his judgment) in extremes:
So over violent or over civil
That every man with him was God or Devil.
In squand'ring wealth was his peculiar art:
Nothing went unrewarded, but desert.
Beggar'd by fools, whom still he found too late:
He had his jest, and they had his estate.

THE POET THOMAS SHADWELL

. . . The midwife laid her hand on his thick skull,
With this prophetic blessing—*Be thou dull;*
Drink, swear, and roar, forbear no lewd delight,
Fit for thy bulk, do anything but write.
Thou art of lasting make, like thoughtless men,
A strong nativity—but for the pen;
Eat opium, mingle arsenic in thy drink,
Still thou mayst live, avoiding pen and ink.
I see, I see 'tis counsel given in vain,
For treason botcht in rhyme will be thy bane;
Rhyme is the rock on which thou art to wreck,
'Tis fatal to thy fame and to thy neck.

FRAGMENT OF A CHARACTER OF JACOB TONSON, HIS PUBLISHER

With leering looks, bull-fac'd, and freckl'd fair,
With two left legs, and Judas-colour'd hair,
And frousy pores that taint the ambient air.

FOOLS IN ENGLAND

Fools change in England, and new fools arise;
For, though th' immortal species never dies,
Yet ev'ry year new maggots make new flies. . . .

AT NATURE'S EARLY BIRTH

In Saturn's reign, at nature's early birth,
There was that thing call'd chastity on earth,
When in a narrow cave, their common shade,
The sheep, the shepherds and their gods were laid:
When reeds and leaves, and hides of beasts were spread
By mountain huswifes for their homely bed,
And mossy pillows rais'd, for the rude husband's head.
Unlike the niceness of our modern dames
(Affected nymphs with new affected names),
The Cynthias and the Lesbias of our years,
Who for a sparrow's death dissolve in tears,
Those first unpolisht matrons, big and bold,
Gave suck to infants of gigantic mould;
Rough as their savage lords who rang'd the wood,
And fat with acorns belcht their windy food.
For when the world was buxom, fresh, and young,
Her sons were undebauch'd, and therefore strong;
And whether born in kindly beds of earth,
Or struggling from the teeming oaks to birth,
Or from what other atoms they begun,
No sires they had, or if a sire the Sun. . . .

84

THE FLOOD

Th' expanded waters gather on the plain,
They float the fields, and over-top the grain;
Then rushing onwards, with a sweepy sway,
Bear flocks, and folds, and lab'ring hinds away.
Nor safe their dwellings were; for, sapped by floods,
Their houses fell upon their household gods.
The solid piles, too strongly built to fall,
High o'er their heads, behold a watry wall:
Now seas and earth were in confusion lost;
A world of waters, and without a coast.
      One climbs a cliff; one in his boat is borne,
And ploughs above, where late he sow'd his corn.
Others o'er chimney tops and turrets row,
And drop their anchors on the meads below:
Or downward driv'n, they bruise the tender vine,
Or tost aloft, are knock't against a pine.
And where of late the kids had cropt the grass,
The monsters of the deep now take their place.
Insulting Nereids on the cities ride,
And wondring dolphins o'er the palace glide.
On leaves and masts of mighty oaks they brouse.
And their broad fins entangle in the boughs.
The frightened wolf now swims amongst the sheep;
The yellow lion wanders in the deep. . . .

JOHN DRYDEN

ALL, ALL OF A PIECE THROUGHOUT

All, all of a piece throughout:
    Thy chase had a beast in view;
Thy wars brought nothing about;
    Thy lovers were all untrue.
'Tis well an old age is out,
    And time to begin a new . . .

WHOM DEATH HAS DOOM'D TO EVERLASTING SLEEP

. . . Why are we then so fond of mortal life,
Beset with dangers, and maintain'd with strife?
A life, which all our care can never save;
One fate attends us; and one common grave.
Besides, we tread but a perpetual round;
We ne'er strike out, but beat the former ground,
And the same mawkish joys in the same track are found.
For still we think an absent blessing best,
Which cloys, and is no blessing when possest;
A new arising wish expels it from the breast.
The fev'rish thirst of life increases still;
We call for more and more, and never have our fill;
Yet know not what tomorrow we shall try,
What dregs of life in the last draught may lie:
Nor, by the longest life we can attain,
One moment from the length of death we gain;
For all behind belongs to his eternal reign.
When once the Fates have cut the mortal thread,
The man as much to all intents is dead,
Who dies today, and will as long be so,
As he who died a thousand years ago.

Christopher Smart   *From the painting in The Hall, Pembroke College, Cambridge*

SEVEN

Christopher Smart
(*1722-1771*)

Christopher Smart lived at first in Kent, where there were sandstone rocks, trees, streams, ponds, in a speckled landscape not far from Sevenoaks, on an estate his father managed for an aristocratic landlord.

In the ponds, to his delight, crucians or golden carp glittered like metal. Such glitterings pleased him all his life, when it was black and sad and when it was happy and filled with sunlight. In Kent he used to walk by the Medway, flowing slowly through hop-fields; he noticed how the silveriness of the river reflected the hops (and in May the cowslips), how silvery bleak and perch glided in the water or broke its polish.

Streams kissed the grass, the sun shone on the leaves of trees, and the noise of the leaves in the wind made Christopher Smart think of Orpheus, the first of poets, who was taught by the Muses so well that everything in the wild, from rock to waterfall, bird to wolf and lion, listened to him when he sang his songs, to his own music on the lyre.

Orpheus became something of a hero to Christopher Smart, and perhaps in the very end, after asylum and madness and loneliness and prison for debt, he may have thought how much he and Orpheus were alike: by his singing Orpheus charmed his way into hell, charmed iron tears from the eyes of Pluto, the Lord of Hell, but even then failed to bring his dead Eurydice back to the happy surface of his world. And his music and his songs could not save him from his own very cruel death, from a savage rout of women who tore him to bits, as the world may tear any poet to bits, by attack or neglect.

All the same the story does say that the Muses, Mothers of Song, collected all the remains of Orpheus's body, and buried them; it does say that the nightingales—birds which are the symbols of poetry—sang over them in the night; and that the Muses took his lyre up into heaven, hanging it there as the constellation of Lyra, which shines above our heads (almost exactly above them) in the delightful weeks of midsummer. Poems, in other words, live on and glitter, after poets die.

Smart lived in this Orpheus land of Kent, at Shipbourne, for his first eleven years. Then his father died, and in 1733 the family moved to a much bleaker countryside in the north, in County Durham, where the noble family of the Vanes, whom his father had served in Kent, had their headquarters, at Raby Castle.

Here he had his first experience of love, which he never forgot. He fell in love with Anne Vane, the daughter of Lord Barnard, at the castle, and the two of them tried to run away. Years later, when he was in an asylum, writing a long rather mad poem, or daily notebook, of praise, he remembered how Anne Vane had blushed when he looked at her during service in the church at Staindrop, near Raby Castle:

For I saw a blush in Staindrop Church, which was of
    God's own colouring.
For it was the benevolence of a virgin shewn to me before
    the whole congregation.

At school in Durham, and then as an undergraduate at Cambridge, a small, sensitive, gay, amused, amusing, even clowning boy, Christopher Smart showed himself clever. He had a rich patron behind him (Lord Barnard and the Vanes easily forgave the elopement), and should, or at any rate, could, have had a comfortable, ordinary, successful life—in the world's eye.

I think his father's death, and the loss to him in childhood of Kent and the crucians and the familiar sparkling and exciting landscape, made him feel that he had lost his real life. Then later he lost his Anne Vane. It was a series of deprivations, and when he became a man nothing quite satisfied him. He felt that his smallness—he called himself an "amorous dwarf" in one poem—made him inferior to people around him of more usual size. He could not settle down to a scholarly life at the university. Perhaps in one way he wanted to be like other people. But the scholars, the men of learning, were heavy, pompous, and censorious, or were thin, dry, and censorious; and ridiculous either way. There was better company in Cambridge ale-houses than in Cambridge colleges.

Smart buffooned and drank and showed off and ran into debt. In London there would be more fun. So to London he moved, and made his living by clever journalism. He wrote anything that was required, in a very conventional way, squibs, funny pieces, songs—songs that had nothing to do with Kent or Orpheus or the glitter of golden carp, or with anything at all which was genuine and worth while inside himself.

Small or no, irresponsible or no, Christopher did marry his publisher's stepdaughter, a girl beautiful, it seems, and golden-haired:

> I'll throw down my pipe, and neglect all my flocks
> And will sing to my lass with the golden locks.

But his career so far was not at all what had been expected of him by his own family or by the Vanes, who had helped him to Cambridge. More debt, more drink. London as difficult as Cambridge: more worry, more confusion. The troubles worked in his mind as if they were maggots inside an apple. He would be full of remorse. He would feel queer in his head, he would recover, amend, fall again into just the same difficulties, and then into the same queerness of the head, the same state of terrors inside a darkness.

When he was remorseful he prayed. When he felt his mind going he prayed against perils and darknesses. When he recovered he felt full of gratitude, he opened the Psalms, and praying turned into praise—Praise the Lord, O my soul—in verse:

> Brisk leaps the heart, the mind's at large once more,
> To love, to praise, to bless, to wonder and adore.

This was how Christopher Smart, half mad, half sane, came in a way face to face with his true self, making in praise—by means of every sparkling thing he had known and loved and admired—that kind of poetry at last which was proper to him, instead of the kind which a poet was supposed to write according to the fashions of the day.

But his madness made him violent, so he found himself shut up by his family in London madhouses. It showed itself in peculiar ways. His habit of praying when he felt madness coming on him was rather like swallowing a tablet or giving oneself an injection before an attack of some bodily illness, except that he prayed and praised, in public, anywhere, in a loud voice.

This little man would take to his knees and his prayers, and his praise, in the theater, in the street (for instance, in crowded Pall Mall), in St. James's Park. He would go to his friends' houses when they were having dinner or in the middle of the night when they were in bed, and call to them that they must come out and praise and pray. He would even climb up and kneel and pray on the roof of some neat, sensible, orderly eighteenth-century house, since he felt that the ceiling indoors was an obstacle between a man's head and God's blessing.

He would pray in the rain, naked. Rain, he said, made the body fresh and pure.

Half sane, half mad, he felt that he was a prophet who was going to bring all the people of England back to praising God. And since the Psalms were the great book of praise for Christians, he determined to make all the hundred and fifty psalms into new English poems.

Smart believed a theory that Orpheus, poet of all poets in Greek myth, had really been King David, the Psalmist of Israel. Little by little, in madness, in sanity, in madness again, in and out of his madhouses, in Shoreditch and in Chelsea, he turned David's psalms into Christopher Smart's poetry. When he had finished, still in the madhouse at Chelsea (it was near Cheyne Walk, by the Thames), he wrote a psalm of his own, "A Song to David," a great towering burst of fireworks to "the best poet who ever lived," as he called David, full of the sparkling wonders he had recalled from his reading and from the happiness of his life in Kent and in County Durham when he was a boy.

Fireworks climb into a black sky, flame, sparkle, and go out; and the blackness returns. The fireworks of this "Song to David" still hang and burst and flame in the mind in sparkling shapes, though it is now more than two hundred years since Christopher Smart put his match to the words, half in lunacy.

So a great poem was made. All that one fashionable poet could say about it, when Smart managed to get it printed after his release in 1763, was: "I have seen his Song to David, and from thence conclude him as mad as ever."

When he was confined at Chelsea, Smart had been treated sometimes well, sometimes badly. He had been worked on with irons, he had been in a damp cell or dungeon, he had been allowed to help in the garden, where he enjoyed growing pinks or carnations. Sometimes he had been deprived of pen and ink. This happened at a time when some of the stanzas of "A Song to David" had been shaping in his head. Having no other way of writing them down, Smart scratched them on the wainscot or wooden panelling of his room with the end of a key.

After he was free, he led a sad, lonely existence. He had nothing more to do with his wife and children. He lived by himself, in London, overlooking St. James's Park, where he had once prayed on his knees so very loudly. He worked and worked, and wrote and wrote, yet at last, in 1717, died under arrest for debt, a poet almost forgotten, though only forty-eight years old.

One girl remembered him sadly, young Fanny Burney, the novelist. Eighteen months before, in the flowerless autumn, he had called on her father. She wrote then in her diary: "Poor Mr. Smart presented me this morning with a rose, blooming and sweet as if we were in the month of June. 'It was given me,' said he, 'by a fair lady—though not so fair as *you*.' "

ADORATION
(FROM A SONG TO DAVID)

For ADORATION all the ranks
Of angels yield eternal thanks,
 And DAVID in the midst;
With God's good poor, which, last and least
In man's esteem, thou to thy feast,
 O blessed bridegroom, bidst.

For ADORATION seasons change,
And order, truth, and beauty range,
 Adjust, attract, and fill:
The grass the polyanthus cheques,
And polish'd porphyry reflects,
 By the descending rill.

Rich almonds colour to the prime
For ADORATION; tendrils climb,
 And fruit-trees pledge their gems;
And Ivis, with her gorgeous vest,
Builds for her eggs her cunning nest,
 And bell-flowers bow their stems.

With vinous syrup cedars sprout;
From rocks pure honey gushing out,
 For ADORATION springs:
All scenes of painting crowd the map
Of nature; to the mermaid's pap
 The scalèd infant clings.

The spotted ounce and playsome cubs
Run rustling 'mongst the flow'ring shrubs,
   And lizards feed the moss;
For ADORATION beasts embark,
While waves upholding halcyon's ark
   No longer roar and toss. . . .

CHRISTMAS DAY

Nature's decorations glisten
   Far above their usual trim;
Birds on box and laurels listen,
   As so near the cherubs hymn.

Boreas now no longer winters
   On the desolated coast;
Oaks no more are riv'n in splinters
   By the whirlwind and his host.

Spinks and ouzels sing sublimely,
   'We too have a Saviour born,'
Whiter blossoms burst untimely
   On the blest Mosaic thorn. . . .

THE SAINTS UNKNOWN

. . . Stars of the superior class,
Which in magnitude surpass,
From the time they rose and shone,
Have their names and places known.

Mazaroth his circuit runs,
With Arcturus and his sons;
Pleiad twinkles o'er the streams
Of Orion's bolder beams.

But what glories in array
Brighten all the milky way,
Where innumerables vie,
Told alone by God Most High!

PRAYER AND PRAISE

Pray'r and praise be mine employment,
　　Without grudging or regret,
Lasting life, and long enjoyment,
　　Are not here, and are not yet.

Hark! aloud, the blackbird whistles,
　　With surrounding fragrance blest,
And the goldfinch in the thistles
　　Makes provision for her nest.

Ev'n the hornet hives his honey,
　　Bluecap builds his stately dome,
And the rocks supply the coney
　　With a fortress and an home.

But the servants of their Saviour,
　　Which with gospel peace are shod,
Have no bed but what the paviour
　　Makes them in the porch of God. . . .

THE STRONG
FROM A SONG TO DAVID

Strong is the horse upon his speed;
Strong in pursuit the rapid glede,
　　Which makes at once his game:
Strong the tall ostrich on the ground;
Strong through the turbulent profound
　　Shoots xiphias to his aim.

Strong is the lion—like a coal
His eyeball—like a bastion's mole
　　His chest against the foes:
Strong, the gier-eagle on his sail,
Strong against tide, th' enormous whale
　　Emerges as he goes.

But stronger still in earth and air,
And in the sea, the man of pray'r,
　　And far beneath the tide;
And in the seat to faith assign'd,
Where ask is have, where seek is find,
　　Where knock is open wide. . . .

William Blake   *Reproduced by permission of the Syndics of the Fitzwilliam Museum, Cambridge*

EIGHT

William Blake

(*1757-1827*)

Respectable, ordinary, satisfied people, even other artists and poets, even some great poets, thought that William Blake was mad—not in the way Christopher Smart had been, but certainly queer or touched.

For one thing, he had a brilliant eye, and he went through London and through life by his own path; he had his own thoughts, he printed his own books in color, as no other books had ever been printed. Also he was liable to have waking visions—to see in front of him (as he looked, according to his phrase, not with his eye, but through it) beings of great imaginative concern to himself, whether they were angels, or the hard Man who built the Pyramids, or the cruel and bloodthirsty Ghost of a Flea (which he painted).

Another thing, William Blake was not for sale. Artists in Blake's London painted what they were told to paint by rich patrons and peers. "The enquiry in England," Blake wrote down angrily in the margin of one of his books, "is not whether a man has talents and genius, but whether he is passive and polite and a virtuous ass and obedient to Noblemen's opinions in art and science. If he is, he is a good man. If not, he must be starved."

By contrast no one could buy William Blake, or hire him, or bend him. If he was not starved, he was always very poor, and he was content to live quietly as a journeyman engraver.

In London (and Blake was decidedly a Londoner) you can still see a few of the houses Blake lived in. But it is a pity that builders in 1963 pulled down the little white corner house of 28 Broad Street (now Broadwick Street), at the back of Oxford Street, because this was the house in which he was born on November 27, 1757, above his father's hosiery shop, and in which he lived as a boy.

Here Blake screamed when he was four years old, because God "put his head to the window"; here, coming back from a walk at Peckham Rye, on the other side of the Thames, he told his surprised father, who nearly beat him for telling lies, that he had just seen "a tree filled with angels, bright angelic wings bespangling every bough like stars."

When he was thirteen, and still living in Broad Street with his brothers and sister, he wrote the poem which begins "How sweet I roam'd from field to field" (on page 111), and it was not long before Blake began to send pictures to the Royal Academy exhibition, and married, and set up a business as printseller and engraver, at No. 27 in the same street, next door to his old home. Here he taught his young wife, who had signed the marriage register with her mark, to read and write. She was to be his help, and his comfort for forty-five years.

Blake's next remove was to a house a few hundred yards away in Poland Street. It has been pulled down and rebuilt. All the same this is a street, a rather narrow and nowadays rather a squalid one, to be looked at with some awe, since it was here that Blake, in the intervals of engraving for publishers and drawing and painting, wrote some of the most magical-seeming and famous of poems in our language.

One was "Ah Sunflower! weary of Time" (on page 114), a second was "Hear the Voice of the Bard" (page 112), and a third was "The Tiger," which everybody knows, that tiger burning bright in the forests of the night. For Blake it was more than a beast glowing with stripes and eyes of fire. I think it was the tiger in him, in this young poet in London, also in each of us, so bright that it might have jumped out of the sun, a fiery delight and energy and fierceness and "wrath," as Blake would say, something wonderful which we have, though we do not always realize that we have it.

From now on, in everything he designed, everything he wrote, Blake concerned himself with mankind in this life, in this world, in this London, which was all the world contracted into one place. He considered the repressions which hold men down and will not allow them to live in energy and freedom and delight of mind.

Every force in our lives he examined and criticized, including that God who had put his head to the windowpane in Broad Street and frightened him so much when he was a child. We make our own handcuffs, we make our own prisons, he thought, and we shut ourselves up inside them. Blake walked down from his engraving room, from his wife Catherine, still a little puzzled by her life with a man so unusual and so absorbed, and out into a grimy self-sold world which began at his door-step. "I wander thro' each charter'd street" (first of all he wrote "dirty street," and "dirty Thames," then changed "dirty" to "chartered," i.e. for hire)—

> I wander thro' each charter'd street,
> Near where the charter'd Thames does flow
> And mark in every face I meet
> Marks of weakness, marks of woe.

In every cry of every Man,
In every Infant's cry of fear,
In every voice, in every ban,
The mind-forg'd manacles I hear.

This young poet, short and broad, with flaming, curling fair hair, and a full forehead, and very large and most intent eyes, did not look at things around him for themselves, he was not in any way a "nature poet": he looked at things, or remembered them, for what they could suggest to him about mankind:

For double the vision my eyes do see
And a double vision is always with me
With my inward eye, 'tis an old Man grey;
With my outward a Thistle across my way.

One day in 1810 (when Blake was now living at South Molton Street, off Bond Street, on the first floor at No. 17, which has a plaque on the wall announcing that Blake lived there) he wrote down in his notebook: "23 May, 1810, found the word Golden." I do not quite understand the date, because he had found the adjective long ago. Perhaps it suddenly struck him how much "golden" was a favorite word, and how very much it contained his meanings.

There are many "golden" things in his poems, whether summer in a golden tent, or the sunflower, or thunder with golden hoofs. Gold, the soft, pure, beautiful, uncommon metal, needs no polish. After centuries a golden object will come out of the soil still yellow and fresh-looking. So, for Blake, gold is something good in our world and in ourselves.

Yet all the same Blake considered this wonderful gold was something too limited, too soft, too natural: it was not as wonderful as gold on fire, burning gold, the golden fire of our minds, the golden sun of our imagination.

Blake thought of Satan, who was not the sun. To him Satan was our wrongness, or error. Satan carried a bow, and it was a black bow. The bow that he, William Blake, was to bend, when he came to write of building "Jerusalem" in England's green and pleasant land ("Jerusalem" meaning all truth, all liberty, all brotherhood, all forgiveness, all imagination, everything holy in men)—this bow was one, not just of gold, but of *gold on fire,* or gold turned into fire.

So if you go down South Molton Street, a little chasm now of hatshops and fashion-houses and coffee-bars and art galleries, think of it as the street of William Blake in which he wrote:

> Bring me my bow of burning gold:
> Bring me my arrows of desire:
> Bring me my spear: O clouds unfold!
> Bring me my chariot of fire.

Proclaiming once that the "outward creation," the ordinary world we live in, wasn't any part of him, but was like the dirt on his shoe, Blake imagined someone immediately protesting, and saying: "What! when the sun rises, do you not see a round disk of fire somewhat like a guinea?"—like a gold coin, in other words. Blake's answer was: "O no, no, I see an innumerable company of the heavenly host, crying, Holy, Holy, Holy is the Lord Almighty." That is to say, the sun rising over London (always rising, never setting) seemed to him that golden fire of our minds, the very best about us, the godly and creative inside us.

Blake heard things, too, which other people never heard, as well as seeing them. Before the rising of the golden sun in the morning over the roofs of London, he used to hear the music of harps sounding through the sky.

His secret was to put wonder of that kind into his poems, in the simplest unaffected words which he locked into rhythms very strong and delicate, very memorable and delightful. Yet though his verses have so much goldenness and morning light about them, Blake could be angry and scornful, especially when he thought of artists who sold their talent and faked, and painted nothing but portraits, like Sir Joshua Reynolds:

> When Sir Joshua Reynolds died
> All Nature was degraded;
> The King dropped a tear into the Queen's ear,
> And all his pictures faded,

or when he thought of the printseller and publisher R. H. Cromek, who cheated him:

> Cromek loves artists as he loves his meat.
> He loves the art, but 'tis the art to cheat.
>
> .   .   .   .
>
> A pretty sneaking knave I knew—
> O Mr Cromek, how do ye do?

All his life Blake wanted us to be honest about our good and our bad, our black and white, our contradictions or contraries, he wanted us to know ourselves so that what was good, true, imaginative, eternal, and he would say divinely human in each of us, would be freed.

Thinking he must be touched in the head, few would listen, few would look at his pictures, or read more than one or two of his poems.

Catherine, though, always helped him. Blake would ask his Muses to come down into his hand, down the nerves of his right arm from his brain, to come down which was the Paradise of the "Eternal Great Humanity Divine"; and when they did this in the rooms in South Molton Street or wherever else Blake and Catherine lived, when words and ideas erupted in him, without regard to the clock, Catherine would sit by her husband. "She would get up in the night, when he was under his very fierce inspirations, which were as if they would tear him asunder, while he was yielding himself to the Muse, or whatever else it would be called, sketching and writing. And so terrible a task did this seem to be, that she had to sit motionless and silent; only to stay him mentally, without moving hand or foot: this for hours, and night after night."

When he was old and even more disregarded by all the established painters and writers of London, living with Catherine, a lonely couple now in a couple of rooms on the first floor of a house in a small courtyard between Fleet Street and the Thames, a group of young artists came to know him, love him, and listen to him as though he were a patriarch or a prophet.

The artist among them who mattered, painting landscape on the country side of the Thames as it might have looked if the hills had been hills of Paradise, and not hills of Kent, was Samuel Palmer, a Bloomsbury bookseller's son.

When he was nineteen, Palmer had been taken by John Linnell (the artist who drew the likeness of Blake on page 100) to meet Blake for the first time.

On Saturday, 9th October, 1824, Mr Linnell called and went with me to Mr Blake. We found him lame in bed of a scalded foot (or leg). There not inactive, though sixty-seven years old, but hard-working on a bed covered with books sat he up like one of the antique patriarchs, or a dying Michael Angelo. Thus and thus was he making in the leaves of a great book (folio) the sublimest designs from his (not superior) Dante. He said he began them with fear and trembling. I said "O! I have enough of fear and trembling." "Then," said he, "you'll do

. . ." And there, first, with fearfulness (which had been the more, but that his designs from Dante had wound me up to forget myself), did I show him some of my first essays in design; and the sweet encouragement he gave me (for Christ blessed little children) did not tend basely to presumption and idleness, but made me work harder and better that afternoon and night. And after visiting him, the scene recurs to me afterwards in a kind of vision; and in this most false, corrupt, and genteelly stupid town my spirit sees his dwelling (the chariot of the sun), as it were an island in the midst of the sea—such a place is it for primitive grandeur, whether in the persons of Mr and Mrs Blake, or in the things hanging on the walls.

Blake talked to these young men of everything, very warmly and electrically. They would kiss his door handle when they came or left, and in their loving respect for this great man they scarcely noticed the shabbiness of his rooms and the poverty of his life (telling one of them that at the moment there wasn't any soap or water in the rooms, Mrs. Blake added: "You see, Mr. Blake's skin don't dirt.").

When Blake died on August 12, 1827, a month or two short of seventy, these young painters saw to his quiet funeral in Bunhill Fields. One of them closed the lids over his gray eyes, which had been so brilliant, so clear, so intent, so flashing with his genius, so sympathetic and melting, and so terrible when he was roused; and which had seen things stranger and more fiery than come into the view of most of us.

All his life long, through Queen Victoria's reign, which may have been an age of greatness and great changes but was yet the most self-sold age in our history, Samuel Palmer remembered Blake as "a man without a mask," happy, never double-minded. In our time another poet, a very different one, T. S. Eliot, said about this unfrightened, always undistracted poet that "he was naked, and saw man naked, and from the centre of his own crystal."

If ever you go looking for Blake and Blake's homes in London, do not miss one contact which is to be had with him, though he has been dead so long. Go to the National Portrait Gallery (next to the National Gallery), and look at the life-mask of Blake. A man who believed in the odd theory that a man's gifts and character can be told by the shape of his head, made it when Blake was old, in 1823. The feel of the wet plaster of the mold on his face caused Blake to set his jaw rather obstinately, in a way that destroyed a sweetness which men noticed about his mouth. But this cast from the mold is Blake—white plaster of Paris or no, it is the head, the delicate structure, the patterning of veins, of one of the greatest of poets.

To see it can cause feelings of reverence and wonder, if you are moved by Blake's poems.

TO THE EVENING STAR

Thou fair-hair'd angel of the evening,
Now, whilst the sun rests on the mountains, light
Thy bright torch of love; thy radiant crown
Put on, and smile upon our evening bed!
Smile on our loves, and, while thou drawest the
Blue curtains of the sky, scatter thy silver dew
On every flower that shuts its sweet eyes
In timely sleep. Let thy west wind sleep on
The lake; speak silence with thy glimmering eyes,
And wash the dusk with silver. Soon, full soon,
Dost thou withdraw; then the wolf rages wide,
And the lion glares thro' the dun forest:
The fleeces of our flocks are cover'd with
Thy sacred dew: protect them with thine influence.

SONG

How sweet I roam'd from field to field,
　　And tasted all the summer's pride,
Till I the prince of love beheld,
　　Who in the sunny beams did glide!

He shew'd me lilies for my hair,
　　And blushing roses for my brow;
He led me through his gardens fair
　　Where all his golden pleasures grow.

With sweet May dews my wings were wet,
　　And Phoebus fir'd my vocal rage;
He caught me in his silken net,
　　And shut me in his golden cage.

He loves to sit and hear me sing,
　　Then, laughing, sports and plays with me;
Then stretches out my golden wing,
　　And mocks my loss of liberty.

INTRODUCTION TO SONGS OF EXPERIENCE

Hear the voice of the Bard!
Who Present, Past, and Future, sees;
Whose ears have heard
The Holy Word
That walk'd among the antient trees,

Calling the lapsèd Soul,
And weeping in the evening dew;
That might control
The starry pole,
And fallen, fallen light renew!

'O Earth, O Earth, return!
Arise from out the dewy grass;
Night is worn,
And the morn
Rises from the slumberous mass.

Turn away no more;
Why wilt thou turn away?
The starry floor,
The wat'ry shore,
Is giv'n thee till the break of day.'

TO THE MUSES

Whether on Ida's shady brow,
    Or in the chambers of the East,
The chambers of the sun, that now
    From antient melody have ceas'd;

Whether in Heav'n ye wander fair,
    Or the green corners of the earth,
Or the blue regions of the air,
    Where the melodious winds have birth;

Whether on chrystal rocks ye rove,
    Beneath the bosom of the sea
Wand'ring in many a coral grove,
    Fair Nine, forsaking Poetry!

How have you left the antient love
    That bards of old enjoy'd in you!
The languid strings do scarcely move!
    The sound is forc'd, the notes are few!

AH! SUN-FLOWER

Ah, Sun-flower! weary of time,
Who countest the steps of the Sun;
Seeking after that sweet golden clime
Where the traveller's journey is done:

Where the Youth pined away with desire,
And the pale Virgin shrouded in snow
Arise from their graves, and aspire
Where my Sun-flower wishes to go.

THE SWORD AND THE SICKLE

The sword sung on the barren heath,
The sickle in the fruitful field:
The sword he sung a song of death,
But could not make the sickle yield.

THE FIENDS OF COMMERCE

Spirit, who lov'st Britannia's Isle
Round which the Fiends of Commerce smile.

William Wordsworth   *Reproduced by permission of the Department of Rare Books, Cornell University Library, Ithaca*

NINE

William Wordsworth
(*1770-1850*)

Poets can look—and usually do look—most unpoetical. If we had come across William Wordsworth in the street when he was in his twenties, we should certainly have glanced at him twice, but I think we should have guessed him to have been a farmer's son, rather out of place on a pavement.

His clothes would have looked as though he did not care where he bought them or how he wore them, though otherwise they would have been ordinary enough. We should have noticed how he walked, how he went down the street with a roll and a plunge, as though he were plodding along a field behind horses and a plow.

If he had stopped to look in the window of a bookshop, we might have been surprised, thinking that such a figure could have no interest in reading, though we might have been less sure if he had turned and we had seen, above his narrow sloping shoulders, the very strong peculiarity of his face, which was long and sallow and divided for most of its length by an exceptionally tall nose, or if we had heard his voice, which was a bit provincial, but exceptionally deep, throaty, and deliberate.

Inquiry might have discovered that this strong but long-nosed oddity, whose hair needed cutting and brushing, was in fact a well-educated young man from the north of England, whose father had been an attorney, and who had just taken his degree at Cambridge. Something about his horseface might have suggested a violent temper or very deep feelings underneath. But even then I think we should never have dreamed that this still quite obvious countryman could have had the fineness of emotion and the power of language required to make him, within a few years, one of the grandest of English poets.

Something, though, might have happened: we might have made some remark, Wordsworth might have seen something, and suddenly the full mouth under his nose and across his solemn horse-face would have started quivering and then have broken into the most enchanting and most human of smiles.

That was the characteristic Wordsworth, and we should have changed our opinion.

Dorothy Wordsworth thought of that smile, which a friend described as "a convulsive inclination to laughter about the mouth," when she waited to see her brother, in 1793, after he had been away for several years. They had only met now and again since they were children. Their mother had died, then their father; they had been separated. Wordsworth had been sent off to school among the lakes and small mountains and honeysuckle-covered trees of the Lake District, and had then gone on to the university.

Now, twenty-three years old, he was coming back from revolutionary France, and Dorothy Wordsworth sat down in her uncle's rectory—she was a year younger, twenty-two—to write to her best friend and describe for her this wonderful favorite brother she was to meet again.

He had all the virtues, but she did have to warn her friend that "his person" was not "in his favor"; she had to admit that he certainly was "rather plain." But, when he began to speak, that smile, which she found "very pleasing," that smile everyone was to know, often lit up a face, she wrote, which seemed to her "extremely thoughtful."

Extraordinary years followed for this brother and sister. She left her rectory, and they set up house together. They lived in exquisite countryside, in the West of England, then among the Lakes. They walked, they were out in all weather, the large, plain poet and the small, plain sister, who was sallow or brown in the face like her brother, a small, quick, gypsy-like girl.

She was gay, he was serious, except when his serious mouth started to break up in laughter. She was all eyes and ears and feeling, he was all thought and passion.

They lived a very ordinary life, which Dorothy described day by day in her journal ("A cold dark morning. William chopped wood—I brought it in a basket. A cold wind"). But they made their ordinary life extraordinary by seeing everything and being aware of everything—which is the way to live.

Dorothy pointed out to William how the leaves shone after rain—wide leaves with broader light, narrow leaves with sparkles of light. William enticed her out when she had a toothache to watch the planet Jupiter spangling the dark sky above a black mountain. She would transplant snowdrops or honeysuckle; he would skate, would give his body to the wind on the black ice of the lake. They had visits from Coleridge, poet of the wonders of "Kubla Khan," who talked like a spring bubbling magically out of the ground, who had read everything, who was their own age, and who noticed everything, like themselves, whether it was white dandelion seeds floating, like life, across a valley or a tear in his child's eye catching the moonlight.

Dorothy Wordsworth found that her brother had grown into someone very passionate, who brooded, yet had control of himself.

This strong brother had once—and only once—been drunk, when he was a student at Cambridge. Why? Because he was spending the evening in the college which Milton had lived in, and was so excited by thinking of Milton and his "keen eye" and his "courageous look" and his "conscious step of purity and pride" when he, too, had been an undergraduate at Cambridge a hundred and sixty years before, that he had drunk glass after glass of wine to Milton's memory.

In France, boiling up to revolution, when it seemed that the world was being born again in justice and decency and freedom, this strong brother had fallen utterly in love with a French girl he had been unable to marry, who had borne him a daughter. But, though he had come home, and France and England were at war, he had risked a journey back into France to see this Annette Vallon of his and their child.

In England again, with Dorothy, with Coleridge, he walked and looked and read and wrote poems, was against government by kings and aristocrats, and thought of the troubles of the poor and the driven.

By candlelight in their house in the Dorset hills, as Dorothy mended socks or made tea, he read philosophers who argued for freedom and condemned torture and tyranny and capital punishment. "I know," he wrote, "that the multitude walk in darkness. I would put into each man's hand a lantern to guide him."

By the fire in their cottage in the mountains, when the stars were sharp outside, and reflected in the lakes, this strong, infinitely tender young poet read over his newly written poems to Dorothy, who would make fair copies for him.

Here I shall say something else about the appearance of this solemn plain poet.

Firelight and candlelight showed Dorothy eyes in her brother's head that one of their friends described as "taking on an appearance the most solemn and spiritual it is possible for the human eye to wear." Dorothy's eyes by contrast gleamed wildly, like a small animal's, in her little, tanned, gypsyish face; her brother's eyes, under heavy eyelids, on either side of his dividing wall of a nose, smoldered and were steady and looked as though they belonged to a prophet of the Old Testament. And if the voice that spoke his newly written poems in front of the fire was so throaty and rather northern, it was also clear, deep, slow, solemn, and sometimes majestic; which seems right.

Things Wordsworth saw and heard all around him—a rainbow (page 125), a waterfall (page 126), a hare raising a wet mist in the early sun (page 128), London in the early morning, from Westminster Bridge (page 130), owls hooting across the lakes and torrents screaming down the mountain (page 124)—made him write poems, but it would not do to call Wordsworth a "nature poet." Calm or still, sparkling or grand, things experienced by this peculiar man suggested to him similar states in men, at their best.

When he was a boy, before he began to write poems, the lakes and the mountains and the rocks and the waterfalls and the sparkling sunlight and the sparkling moonlight and the black shadows of the moon filled him with a huge, absorbing delight. When he was older and wrote his best poems in company with Dorothy, he thought about that kind of delight, and what it does to us in our lives.

A shepherd alone in the mountains was a sight Wordsworth frequently saw in his schooldays. Sometimes the shepherd loomed up a few steps away—

> In size a giant, stalking through thick fog,
> His sheep like Greenland bears.

Sometimes a mountain ridge would be all shadow, and on top of it a shepherd would stand alone in the radiance of a sunset. Sometimes he would see a shepherd standing a long way off, "above all height," like a cross for worship. Wordsworth realized later on how fortunate it was to have seen Man first of all in this particular way, "through objects that were great and fair," and not crowded anxiously into cities.

Another time he climbed Snowdon, the highest mountain in Wales, at night, in a summer fog. All of a sudden he was clear of the fog, and he saw a full moon majestically in the sky, above a hundred hills, which heaved their dark backs out of the moonlit mist all around. This he came to think of as a type of majestic, human intellect.

In the end, and when he wrote his greatest poem, *The Prelude,* Wordsworth realized that the Mind of Man becomes

> A thousand times more beautiful than the earth
> On which he dwells,

and he knew that this Mind of Man was his real subject; and giving it those capitals because it can be so majestic, he called it "My haunt, and the main region of my song."

In his Cambridge days, he lay in bed, looking down in the moonlight at the antechapel of Trinity College, thinking of the white marble statue of Sir Isaac Newton inside the antechapel, with a prism in one hand; and thinking of Newton's "silent face." Afterward he described the face as

> The marble index of a mind for ever
> Voyaging through strange seas of thought alone.

That was the Mind of Man, which was the haunt of this poet, who also wrote:

> There is
> One great society alone on earth:
> The noble Living and the noble Dead.

You will find something very determined and straightforward about Wordsworth's poems. They walk forward, in a straight line; and that was how he made them. Poems, you will remember, came to Milton in the early morning, sometimes while he was still in bed (when Milton was twenty-one, he made up his poem, "On the Morning of Christ's Nativity," actually on Christmas morning, at daybreak). Wordsworth, saying them over to himself, liked to make his poems walking up and down a straight path or any smooth place where there was nothing to get in his way or interrupt.

THERE WAS A BOY

There was a Boy; ye knew him well, ye cliffs
And islands of Winander!—many a time,
At evening, when the earliest stars began
To move along the edges of the hills,
Rising or setting, would he stand alone,
Beneath the trees, or by the glimmering lake;
And there, with fingers interwoven, both hands
Pressed closely palm to palm and to his mouth
Uplifted, he, as through an instrument,
Blew mimic hootings to the silent owls,
That they might answer him.—And they would shout
Across the watery vale, and shout again,
Responsive to his call,—with quivering peals,
And long halloos, and screams, and echoes loud
Redoubled and redoubled; concourse wild
Of jocund din! And, when there came a pause
Of silence such as baffled his best skill:
Then, sometimes, in that silence, while he hung
Listening, a gentle shock of mild surprise
Has carried far into his heart the voice
Of mountain-torrents; or the visible scene
Would enter unawares into his mind
With all its solemn imagery, its rocks,
Its woods, and that uncertain heaven received
Into the bosom of the steady lake . . . .

MY HEART LEAPS UP

My heart leaps up when I behold
    A rainbow in the sky:
So was it when my life began;
So is it now I am a man;
So be it when I shall grow old,
    Or let me die!
The Child is father of the Man;
And I could wish my days to be
Bound each to each by natural piety.

IT WAS AN APRIL MORNING

It was an April morning: fresh and clear
The Rivulet, delighting in its strength,
Ran with a young man's speed; and yet the voice
Of waters which the winter had supplied
Was softened down into a vernal tone.
The spirit of enjoyment and desire
And hopes and wishes, from all living things
Went circling, like a multitude of sounds.
The budding groves seemed eager to urge on
The steps of June; as if their various hues
Were only hindrances that stood between
Them and their object: but, meanwhile, prevailed
Such an entire contentment in the air
That every naked ash, and tardy tree
Yet leafless, showed as if the countenance
With which it looked on this delightful day
Were native to the summer.—Up the brook
I roamed in the confusion of my heart,
Alive to all things and forgetting all.
At length I to a sudden turning came
In this continuous glen, where down a rock
The Stream, so ardent in its course before,
Sent forth such sallies of glad sound, that all
Which I till then had heard, appeared the voice
Of common pleasure: beast and bird, the lamb,
The Shepherd's dog, the linnet and the thrush
Vied with this waterfall, and made a song,
Which, while I listened, seemed like the wild growth
Or like some natural produce of the air,

That could not cease to be. Green leaves were here;
But 'twas the foliage of the rocks—the birch,
The yew, the holly, and the bright green thorn,
With hanging islands of resplendent furze:
And, on a summit, distant a short space,
By any who should look beyond the dell,
A single mountain-cottage might be seen.
I gazed and gazed . . . .

ALL THINGS THAT LOVE THE SUN

. . . All things that love the sun are out of doors;
The sky rejoices in the morning's birth;
The grass is bright with rain-drops;—on the moors
The hare is running races in her mirth;
And with her feet she from the plashy earth
Raises a mist; that, glittering in the sun,
Runs with her all the way, wherever she doth run . . . .

THE WORLD IS TOO MUCH WITH US

The world is too much with us; late and soon,
Getting and spending, we lay waste our powers:
Little we see in Nature that is ours;
We have given our hearts away, a sordid boon!
This Sea that bares her bosom to the moon;
The winds that will be howling at all hours,
And are up-gathered now like sleeping flowers;
For this, for every thing, we are out of tune;
It moves us not.—Great God! I'd rather be
A Pagan suckled in a creed outworn;
So might I, standing on this pleasant lea,
Have glimpses that would make me less forlorn;
Have sight of Proteus rising from the sea;
Or hear old Triton blow his wreathèd horn.

LINES WRITTEN IN EARLY SPRING

I heard a thousand blended notes,
While in a grove I sate reclined,
In that sweet mood when pleasant thoughts
Bring sad thoughts to the mind.

To her fair works did Nature link
The human soul that through me ran;
And much it grieved my heart to think
What man has made of man.

Through primrose tufts, in that green bower,
The periwinkle trailed its wreaths;
And 'tis my faith that every flower
Enjoys the air it breathes.

The birds around me hopped and played,
Their thoughts I cannot measure:—
But the least motion which they made,
It seemed a thrill of pleasure.

The budding twigs spread out their fan,
To catch the breezy air;
And I must think, do all I can,
That there was pleasure there.

If this belief from heaven be sent,
If such be Nature's holy plan,
Have I not reason to lament
What man has made of man?

COMPOSED UPON WESTMINSTER BRIDGE, SEPT. 3, 1802

Earth has not any thing to show more fair:
Dull would he be of soul who could pass by
A sight so touching in its majesty:
This City now doth, like a garment, wear
The beauty of the morning; silent, bare,
Ships, towers, domes, theatres, and temples lie
Open unto the fields, and to the sky;
All bright and glittering in the smokeless air.
Never did sun more beautifully steep
In his first splendour, valley, rock, or hill;
Ne'er saw I, never felt, a calm so deep!
The river glideth at his own sweet will:
Dear God! the very houses seem asleep;
And all that mighty heart is lying still!

AFTER-THOUGHT
(*To the River Duddon*)

I thought of Thee, my partner and my guide,
As being past away.—Vain sympathies!
For, backward, Duddon! as I cast my eyes,
I see what was, and is, and will abide;
Still glides the Stream, and shall for ever glide;
The Form remains, the Function never dies;
While we, the brave, the mighty, and the wise,
We Men, who in our morn of youth defied
The element, must vanish;—be it so!
Enough, if something from our hands have power
To live, and act, and serve the future hour;
And if, as toward the silent tomb we go,
Through love, through hope, and faith's transcendent dower,
We feel that we are greater than we know.

John Clare   *From the painting in the National Portrait Gallery*

TEN

John Clare
(*1793-1864*)

John Clare never went to more than a village school, and was rather patronizingly known in his early life as the "Northamptonshire Peasant Poet," the wonder who wrote poems, though he wasn't educated. But education is not everything to a poet. Much of what comes to him at school may educate him away from poems, and he may have to educate himself back into the possibility of making poems, in his own way and his own time. At any rate each poet does have to find himself, and then maintain that self for as long as possible.

In his Northamptonshire village of Helpston, where he was born in 1793, people no doubt thought that John Clare—if they bothered to think about him at all—had no right to be anything except a farm laborer like his father.

Yet a look at Clare might have made them doubt whether he could ever do heavy work. He was small, in which he resembled Christopher Smart, that other poet of madness and praise and sparkle, not large and immensely strong like Tennyson, who never had to live by his strength. He was born a twin (like Vaughan). They had been premature, the twin sister did not survive, and Clare had come into his poor cottage so weak, shriveled, and tiny that his mother thought he could never live to be a man.

The Clares knew real poverty. John Clare's father seldom brought home more than eight shillings a week, and in a village where, from an early age, you worked or starved, Clare worked. He weeded corn, he helped with the hay, he went around from farm to farm with his father, who found autumn and winter employment as a "whop-straw," a thresher, threshing out grain with a heavy wooden flail, the hardest, the dryest, the most hated of farm jobs. Clare worked alongside his father, whacking at the straw with a specially made flail of a size he could manage.

In between he went to the village school, a slip of a creature still, with light blue eyes, the very lightest fair hair (locks of it survive), hands very fine and delicate, a high forehead, and a mind given to fears and hauntings. He saw a man fall off a load of hay and break his neck. For years he could not forget the pallor of the dead face; he used to have fainting fits; and, into the bargain, he was weakened by malaria, which was common in those days in the Fens (and was then known as ague).

His parents looked at him, and thought they had better turn a child so puny into a shoemaker. Clare, though, was not at all unhappy. He found the still unenclosed pastures and commons and even the monotonously sad Fens altogether delicious, altogether sparkling. He liked the burning yellow of marsh marigolds against black earth, he particularly liked the rising of "red and roundy" suns into frosty skies over a flat landscape. Years after, when he was quite sure that writing poems had begun for him in nature and in love, he said quite soberly that he found his poems in the fields and "only wrote them down."

You can see what he meant from a description of himself as a boy, escaping from laboring and school and odd jobs (such as collecting dung for fuel), especially on Sundays—escaping across the common and into the woods:

I lov'd the gipsies for the beauties which they added to the landscape, I heard the cuckoo's wandering voice. . . . I often pull'd my hat over my eyes to watch the rising of the lark or to see the hawk hang in the summer sky and the kite take its wide circles round the wood. I often linger'd a minute on the woodland stile to hear the wood-pigeons clapping their wings among the dark oaks. . . . I lov'd the pasture with its rushes and thistles and sheep tracks. I adored the wild marshy fen with its solitary hern-shaw* sweeping along in its melancholy sky, I wandered the heath in raptures among the rabbit burrows and golden blossom'd furze. . . . I marked the varied colours in flat spreading fields checker'd with closes of different tinted grain like the colours in a map, the copper-tinted colours of clover in blossom, the sun-tanned green of the ripening hay, the light hues of wheat and barley inter-mix'd with the sunny glare of the yellow carlock and the sunset imitation of the scarlet headaches† with the blue cornbottles‡ crowding their splendid colours in large sheets over the land and troubling the cornfields with de-stroying beauty, the different greens of the woodland trees, the dark oak, the paler ash, the mellow lime, the white poplar peeping above the rest like leafy steeples, the grey willow shining chilly in the sun as if the morning mist still lingered on its cool green. I felt the beauty of these with eager delight . . . the dragonflies in spangled coats darting like winged arrows down the thin stream, the swallow darting through its one-arch'd bridge, the shepherd hiding from the thunder-shower in a hol-

* Heron.
† Poppies.
‡ Cornflowers, now very rare in English fields.

low dotterel,* the wild geese skudding along and making all the letters of the alphabet as they flew the motley clouds, the whispering wind that muttered to the leaves and summer grasses, as it flitted among them like things at play: I observ'd all this with the same raptures as I have done since, but I knew nothing of poetry: it was felt and not uttered.

This was the beginning, or more than the beginning, of John Clare's real education, all this "rapture" in existence which he did not have to unlearn; and though he left school at twelve, he quite soon, in fact, discovered something of poetry.

His mother, his father, and an old woman who kept the cows on the common while Clare minded the sheep had sung him ballads and folk songs. He had heard them, too, from gypsies (who taught him to play airs on the violin). Then a year or two years after his schooling was finished, someone in Helpston showed him a copy of Thomson's *Seasons*.

He was surprised to find long poems actually about things he knew, the sun, storms, rain, rainbows, spring, summer, autumn, winter, snow, frost, skating, oak trees, the smell of bean-fields in blossom.

Cadging eighteenpence, he walked one morning into Stamford and bought (there was sixpence change, after all) his own copy of *The Seasons,* and was so excited on the way home through Burghley Park that he sat among the lime trees and wrote down his first considerable poem, which he called "The Morning Walk." He was now fourteen.

Poems, he found, could be made about everything which delighted him, though his spelling and punctuation might not be very sure. If he watched a cuckoo on an oak and noticed that the inside of the cuckoo's mouth, when it opened its bill to sing, was bright red, here was something which could be

* A pollarded tree.

transformed actually into a poem—though the poem might not always complete itself and finish properly. Or climbing an oak after a buzzard's nest, he noticed that the trunk was rain-washed on one side, and covered on the other side with lichen which rubbed off on him, and tasted bitter: here was another poem, or another fragment (see page 141).

Girls occur in fields, as well as other objects of nature. Clare fell in love with a girl, Mary Joyce, whom he never married, seldom or never saw after he was sixteen or seventeen, and never forgot. There were other girls. He fell in and out of love, he married, he had children, yet always he thought of this girl he first loved, who persisted for him like a flower living inside its own perfume. In his mind, love did not drive out nature: the two seemed to combine, love was every delightful object, every delightful object was love. As for poems, Clare said that what made him write "was downright pleasure in giving vent to my feelings."

"I wrote because it pleased me in sorrow and when happy, it makes me happier and so I go on."

Another time he said that the burning of his heart and the pleasures of being alone and "the restless revels" of making poems sapped his memories like the sun, which in the end may—but only for a while—dry up the stream.

In fact, Clare's memories of delight were inexhaustible; and completing his poet's self-education in the proper way, he came to know most of English poetry. Yet everything, or almost everything, went wrong. He was "discovered," his poems were published, he was introduced to London, he became a sensation as the "Northamptonshire Peasant Poet." He was taken up, dropped, neglected, forgotten. He drank. He could settle neither as poet nor in some kind of country labor, nor as husband, nor as father. He suffered from gloom, despondency, remorse, was one morning up, another morning down.

Confusion occupied his head. For a while he was treated in a private asylum in Epping Forest, where he wandered about among the bracken and the trees, staring away to a distant London which looked, he wrote in a poem (since he could still make poems), "like a shrub among the hills." Here in the forest, at High Beech, Clare might have watched the young Tennyson skating on the pond in a long blue cloak, and Tennyson might have looked up and seen Clare between the trees, a stocky, short, middle-aged little man, shabbily dressed, staring at him from his light blue eyes under a tall wide forehead.

One July day in 1841 Clare left, having discovered the direction from a gypsy, and walked eighty miles home into Northamptonshire, penniless, hungry, with blistered feet, in a kind of dream, thinking with one half of his mind that he was walking home to his long lost unforgotten Mary Joyce, whom he hadn't seen for thirty or more years.

Clare was at home for a while with his real wife and their children. Then keepers came one day just after Christmas 1841 and led him off to the public asylum in Northampton. Dr. Skrimshire, the local doctor who signed the papers for his admission, had known Clare for a long while. Without an inkling that this little man he was dealing with was one of the greater poets of England, he wrote down in the form that Clare's madness had come "After years addicted to Poetical prosing."

This was not the end. Clare lived just over twenty-three years in the asylum. He had much freedom to walk into the town or into the fields, but he never tried to escape, as if he realized that he might not be welcome at home, and that the keepers would only come and fetch him again, and keep him this time close and confined.

He was both mad and sane. One of his fellow patients remembered that this little fattening large-headed man seemed "like the King of the Forest," bold and indomitable—"There was a prowess in his limbs and a majesty in his fiery eye."

Sometimes he believed he was Nelson, sometimes Lord Byron, sometimes a champion boxer. But he was also himself, John Clare, poet, who thought on about love and freedom, and wrote poems, and still more poems, a few of them the best he had ever made. He believed, still, that nature was his wife and his mother. He wrote poems about Mary Joyce, he wrote that love had failed him, that love's bed was always snow, yet that love lived beyond death and earth and flowers and dew.

He looked at the Evening Star, the star of love, in the blue heaven over Northampton, and wrote that it told the traveler on his way that "Earth shall be forgiven"; and though he was in an asylum, he felt that he was now eternity's poet, that he was immortal, that immortality began in first love, that he had snatched an eternal ray from the sun and written with it until earth was only a name, written himself into immortality with it, keeping his spirit with the free (the poem is on page 147).

A wonderful pen. It dropped from Clare's hand after a while. He wrote fewer poems; he felt, so he said, as if all the vowels had been picked out through his ears, and at last he died on a warm spring day in 1864, and was sent home in a coffin, taking then his first and only ride in a train.

A stone was put on his grave in Helpston churchyard calling him again, so patronizingly, "John Clare the Northamptonshire Peasant Poet." Afterward, among his papers, there was found Clare's rough drawing of the memorial he would have liked, a rough stone like a milestone, inscribed with this, and no more, no dates, no details:

HERE

Rest the

HOPES

and Ashes

of

JOHN CLARE

THE PUDDOCK'S NEST

The huge oaks' splintered trunks appear
When spring is in her pride
As they were whitewashed every year
Upon their northern side,

And when I clomb the puddock's nest
The side that faced the south
The dust that rubbed off gen my breast
Came bitter in my mouth.

THE CUCKOO

I've watched it on an old oak tree
Sing half an hour away
Until its quick eye noticed me
And then it whewed away.

Its mouth when open shone as red
As hips upon the briar. . . .

FROM SUMMER IMAGES

I love at early morn, from new-mown swath,
    To see the startled frog his route pursue,
And mark while, leaping o'er the dripping path,
    His bright sides scatter dew;
And early lark that from its bustle flies
    To hail his matin new;
        And watch him to the skies:

And note on hedgerow baulks, in moisture sprent,
    The jetty snail creep from the mossy thorn,
With earnest heed and tremulous intent,
    Frail brother of the morn,
That from the tiny bents and misted leaves
    Withdraws his timid horn,
        And fearful vision weaves.

Or swallow heed on smoke-tanned chimney-top,
    Wont to be first unsealing Morning's eye,
Ere yet the bee hath gleaned one wayward drop
    Of honey on his thigh;
To see him seek morn's airy couch to sing,
    Until the golden sky
        Bepaint his russet wing. . . .

SONG: LOVE LIVES BEYOND THE TOMB

> Love lives beyond
> The tomb, the earth, which fades like dew—
> I love the fond,
> The faithful, and the true.
>
> Love lives in sleep,
> The happiness of healthy dreams,
> Eve's dews may weep,
> But love delightful seems.
>
> 'Tis seen in flowers,
> And in the even's pearly dew
> On earth's green hours,
> And in the heaven's eternal blue.
>
> 'Tis heard in spring
> When light and sunbeams, warm and kind,
> On angel's wing
> Bring love and music to the wind.
>
> And where is voice
> So young and beautifully sweet
> As nature's choice,
> When spring and lovers meet?
>
> Love lives beyond
> The tomb, the earth, the flowers, and dew.
> I love the fond,
> The faithful, young, and true.

HESPERUS

Hesperus! the day is gone,
Soft falls the silent dew,
A tear is now on many a flower
And heaven lives in you.

Hesperus! the evening mild
Falls round us soft and sweet.
'Tis like the breathings of a child
When day and evening meet.

Hesperus! the closing flower
Sleeps on the dewy ground,
While dews fall in a silent shower
And heaven breathes around.

Hesperus! thy twinkling ray
Beams in the blue of heaven,
And tells the traveller on his way
That Earth shall be forgiven!

I THINK OF THEE AT EARLY DAY

I think of thee at early day,
And wonder where my love can be;
And when the evening shadows grey,
O how I think of thee!

Along the meadow banks I rove
And down the flaggy fen,
And hope, my first and early love,
To meet thee once agen.

I think of thee at dewy morn
And at the sunny noon,
And walk with thee—now left forlorn—
Beneath the silent moon.

I think of thee, I think of all,
How blest we both have been—
The sun looks pale upon the wall
And autumn shuts the scene.

FROM SOLITUDE

Green solitude, his prison, pleasure yields,
The bitch fox heeds him not; birds seem to laugh.
He lives the Crusoe of his lonely field
Whose dark green oaks his noontide leisure shield.

A VISION

I lost the love of heaven above,
    I spurned the lust of earth below,
I felt the sweets of fancied love,
    And hell itself my only foe.

I lost earth's joys, but felt the glow
    Of heaven's flame abound in me,
Till loveliness and I did grow
    The bard of immortality.

I loved but woman fell away,
    I hid me from her faded fame,
I snatch'd the sun's eternal ray
    And wrote till earth was but a name.

In every language upon earth,
    On every shore, o'er every sea,
I gave my name immortal birth
    And kept my spirit with the free.

Tennyson reading "Maud"   *Reproduced by permission of the*
Museum and Art Gallery, Birmingham

ELEVEN

Alfred Tennyson
(*1809-1892*)

Tennyson may be the poet for you if you are feeling sad, and if on top of that or inside it, or around it, you feel that your sadness is part of a mysterious sadness of everything, of all the human race, of all the things around you, sunset, a wet day in summer, cuckoos, autumn, wind, uplands, church bells, distance, or the sea, or the various noises of waves on the shore.

No poet more wonderfully contrived richer, more angelica-and-cherry-topped, creamier trifles flavored with a liqueur of sadness. But Tennyson is the only Englishman ever to have been raised to a peer of the realm because he wrote poems, and this makes it rather hard to discover the poet who actually wrote the poems, the best ones, behind the beard and the pomp and the noble face of the pictures which were the Official Tennyson.

Real Tennyson grew up in a Lincolnshire rectory, at Somersby, under the wolds, which are rolling sheep pastures. Here he was one of the twelve children—no fewer, though the eldest of them died as a baby—of a tall, at once stern and tender clergyman, who had never wanted to be a clergyman, who was bitter because he had been disinherited by his father, and so was "all his life a man of sorrow and acquainted with grief."

Tennyson, whom his parents and his brothers and sisters, it is a litle hard to imagine, called "Ally," took after his father in some ways. He was always conscious of himself in special, sad situations, deprived, abandoned, alone a noble figure with great distances around him, on a beach (the sad North Sea was fourteen miles away from the rectory, across the fens), on a long, long beach where the tide hissed or waves pounded, or on long rolling windy uplands, at night under the sparkle of Orion. He was very full of himself, he wanted to know why Alfred Tennyson existed, in this rectory at Somersby, son of this almost mad father, who drank, was sometimes violent, and once threatened to kill one of his children; why it was that he existed among these brothers and sisters, in this world; and he would call "Alfred, Alfred, Alfred" to himself out in the dark.

He remembered that before he could read he used to spread his arms to the wind on stormy days and cry out: "I hear a voice that's speaking in the wind," that he was enchanted then (as always) by the words "far, far away," and that the first poetry to move him had been his own, at five years old.

When he was eight he wrote a line,

With slaughterous sons of thunder rolled the flood,

which he would say to himself in a rolling grandeur, sure that it was a better line than Scott, Campbell, or Lord Byron had ever written.

When he was twelve he wrote an epic of six thousand lines about battles and the sea and mountains. Just as he had shouted "Alfred" in the dark, so he would shout lines from the epic out in the fields at night around the rectory.

In this countryside many springs bubble up under sandstone rocks. When Tennyson was fourteen, and the news came to the rectory of Lord Byron's death at Missolonghi, in Greece, all the world seemed dark to this poet for whom Lord Byron was a hero (as he had been to John Clare), and he went out to one of these springs, and cut the words "Byron is dead" into the soft rock.

Since he believed by this time that he was going to be a poet as great and as famous as Byron (his family, including his father, held the same view), what did it matter if a stern aunt staying at the rectory said to him: "Alfred, Alfred, when I look at you I think of the words of Holy Scripture—'Depart from me, ye cursed, into everlasting fire' "? Yet that was almost the way he felt at times: if not exactly condemned and cursed, then cast out, or at any rate marked out for sorrow.

Away at school for four years, from seven to eleven, he was bullied and beaten and very unhappy, and was glad to come back to Somersby and the long, gray fields, and be taught by his father.

He went away to Cambridge as an undergraduate, he made friends, he wrote poems, and his friends admired the poems. But though strong and big, six feet tall, dark-haired, swarthy-skinned, handsome, and successful, Tennyson was still nervous and moody, and fond of being alone—with "sorrow." He caught sights and sounds extraordinarily, once seeing, for instance, the light of the moon on the eye of a nightingale as it sang in the hedgerow. But he was full of fears—about Alfred. One such fear was that he might go blind. He was going to be—or was actually becoming—a great poet: great poets, one of his brothers reminded him, in perceiving "the Inward Sublime" go blind sometimes—like Milton or Homer.

In spite of success, Tennyson did not like being away from home and Lincolnshire. His queer, stern, sad father lapsed into illness, and he was called back from Cambridge to the rectory to watch him die. (Tennyson then did a peculiar thing—before he had been dead for a week he slept in his father's bed, hoping that if he did so he would see his father's ghost.) He did not go back to Cambridge, he never took his degree. The Tennysons—and Alfred too, reading, learning, writing—stayed on in their much-loved rectory for another six years. Then they had to leave, and they came south to the neighborhood of London.

"Me my own Fate to lasting sorrow doometh." So Tennyson began a poem when he was twenty-three. And up to now it had been deprivations all the way. Then, while Tennyson was still at Somersby, still in communion with bare wolds and the long melancholy flat Lincolnshire brims of the sea, still looking after his brothers and sisters, who were most of them rather odd and ineffectual characters, his Cambridge friend Arthur Hallam suddenly died, a deprivation which was to make him write all the poems of *In Memoriam*. It was a deprivation, too, for his favorite sister, who was to have married Hallam.

Also Tennyson had his own difficulty about love and a wife. He had first met the Lincolnshire girl he wanted to marry when she was walking with Arthur Hallam in a wood. It was May, she was seventeen years old, wearing a gray dress, and he asked her, a little affectedly: "Are you a Dryad or an Oread wandering here?"

Six years later, in 1836, he fell in love with her (when he was twenty-seven), and she with him. They met and wrote to each other. But in those days a middle-class marriage on little or no money was out of the question, and Tennyson was too busy deliberately becoming a great poet to make any money. Also these odd Tennysons were a family to look at with some disquiet. After four years his prospects as a husband were no better. Letters were forbidden, and they had to separate. Ten years went by before they met again, and were at last married, Tennyson more than forty (his poems were now selling), his Emily thirty-seven.

Every sorrow, every separation, every deprivation was a bowl for mixing the poems, which were now making him famous. Every sorrow provided Tennyson with a situation in which writing another poem was both a comfort and a piece of glory. Every such situation made him ask again, in his music of words prompted by all his feeling for the wolds and the fens and the waves and the winds and the trees and the streams and the church-bells of his Lincolnshire, made him ask again in poems *Who am I? And why, and again, why do I, Alfred Tennyson of Somersby—and all the rest of mankind— exist?*

A poem often begins with a small string of words which suddenly come together in one's head. The words may be suggested by something seen, heard, smelled, touched, remembered, which fits in with one's feelings at the time. Tennyson said he used to make up a line of four or five words or more about anything that struck him "as picturesque in nature": he would declaim such lines out of doors in the wind (just as he had done when he was eight years old). Sometimes they would float away and he would forget them. "Many and many a line has gone away on the north wind," he said. Sometimes they dovetailed with his feeling, and were made to grow or enlarge into a poem, or they were fitted into some longer poem he was writing.

It must have worked that way in "The Splendour Falls on Castle Walls" (on page 159). He wrote it after he had been rowed round the lakes at Killarney, in Ireland. There comes a point on the row where the boatman blows a bugle to the mountains. Echo brings the bugle call back in a most thrilling way, at once near and distant, clear and dying. I think "dying, dying, dying" or "answer, echoes, dying, dying, dying" were the words which the echo suggested at once to Tennyson, the words which collected other words in his head and grew into the poem.

When a poem was finished, Tennyson liked an audience, he liked reading it to his friends, and (so it seems) they liked to hear him. He rolled it out in a splendid voice, with broad north-country vowels, "very deep and deep chested, but rather murmuring than mouthing, like the sound of a far sea or of a pine-wood."

Imagine that voice when it came to special, very Tennysonian lines: "The mellow ouzel fluted in the elm," "There let the wind sweep and the plover cry," or sea-lines from the flat Lincolnshire shore: "Dim shores, dense rains, and heavy-clouded sea," or "Save for some whisper of the seething seas."

He said he preferred writing in the early spring, when nature begins to wake up. But some of his best poems certainly belong to October or November, like "Calm Is the Morn without a Sound" (page 157), which is a picture from the Lincolnshire wolds and flat fens, or "Tears, Idle Tears," which he wrote at ruined Tintern Abbey when the leaves were yellowing.

In the end they buried Alfred Tennyson very grandly in Westminster Abbey, with seven peers of the realm, including one duke, among the pallbearers. He had had all the fame he wanted (one of his last books sold twenty thousand copies in the first week). He had been made Poet Laureate, and Queen Victoria had created him Lord Tennyson, more for his fame than his poems, or less for his good poems than for the many pompous and silly ones he wrote at times when he forgot Lincolnshire, and filled himself up with the importance of being a Great Public Bellows who was Thinking as Expected—though he was good only at feeling and being sad about himself, not at thinking—and addressing all England and America in platitudes as big as a prime minister's.

One wish he never fulfilled, which was to see the earth or England from a balloon. If he didn't manage this, he did once, when he was twenty-three, have a daydream of Alfred Tennyson aloft; he wrote four stanzas about himself as the great poet sailing in broad, blue midday, above "tilth, hamlet, mead and mound," in the basket of a crimson balloon, waving his flags to the shouting mob below, and rising higher into secret splendors—though in fact he rose higher into that peerage which had nothing at all to do with poetry.

COME NOT, WHEN I AM DEAD

Come not, when I am dead,
    To drop thy foolish tears upon my grave,
To trample round my fallen head,
    And vex the unhappy dust thou wouldst not save.
There let the wind sweep and the plover cry;
       But thou, go by.

Child, if it were thine error or thy crime
    I care no longer, being all unblest:
Wed whom thou wilt, but I am sick of Time,
    And I desire to rest.
Pass on, weak heart, and leave me where I lie:
       Go by, go by.

CALM IS THE MORN WITHOUT A SOUND

Calm is the morn without a sound,
    Calm as to suit a calmer grief,
    And only thro' the faded leaf
The chestnut pattering to the ground:

Calm and deep peace on this high wold,
    And on these dews that drench the furze,
    And all the silvery gossamers
That twinkle into green and gold:

Calm and still light on yon great plain
    That sweeeps with all its autumn bowers,
    And crowded farms and lessening towers,
To mingle with the bounding main:

Calm and deep peace in this wide air,
    These leaves that redden to the fall;
    And in my heart, if calm at all,
If any calm, a calm despair:

Calm on the seas, and silver sleep,
    And waves that sway themselves in rest,
    And dead calm in that noble breast
Which heaves but with the heaving deep. . . .

NOW SLEEPS THE CRIMSON PETAL

Now sleeps the crimson petal, now the white;
Nor waves the cypress in the palace walk;
Nor winks the gold fin in the porphyry font:
The fire-fly wakens: waken thou with me.

Now droops the milk-white peacock like a ghost,
And like a ghost she glimmers on to me.

Now lies the Earth all Danaë to the stars,
And all thy heart lies open unto me.

Now slides the silent meteor on, and leaves
A shining furrow, as thy thoughts in me.

Now folds the lily all her sweetness up,
And slips into the bosom of the lake:
So fold thyself, my dearest, thou, and slip
Into my bosom and be lost in me.

THE SPLENDOUR FALLS ON CASTLE WALLS

The splendour falls on castle walls
    And snowy summits old in story:
The long light shakes across the lakes,
    And the wild cataract leaps in glory.
Blow, bugle, blow, set the wild echoes flying,
Blow, bugle; answer, echoes, dying, dying, dying.

O hark, O hear! how thin and clear,
    And thinner, clearer, farther going!
O sweet and far from cliff and scar
    The horns of Elfland faintly blowing!
Blow, let us hear the purple glens replying:
Blow, bugle; answer, echoes, dying, dying, dying.

O love, they die in yon rich sky,
    They faint on hill or field or river:
Our echoes roll from soul to soul
    And grow for ever and for ever.
Blow, bugle, blow, set the wild echoes flying,
And answer, echoes, answer, dying, dying, dying.

LINES

Here often, when a child, I lay reclined,
 I took delight in this locality.
Here stood the infant Ilion of the mind,
 And here the Grecian ships did seem to be.
And here again I come, and only find
 The drain-cut levels of the marshy lea,—
Gray sandbanks, and pale sunsets,—dreary wind,
 Dim shores, dense rains, and heavy-clouded sea!

FRATER AVE ATQUE VALE

Row us out from Desenzano, to your Sirmione row!
So they row'd, and there we landed—'O venusta Sirmio!'
There to me thro' all the groves of olive in the summer glow,
There beneath the Roman ruin where the purple flowers
    grow,
Came that 'Ave atque Vale' of the Poet's hopeless woe,
Tenderest of Roman poets nineteen hundred years ago,
'Frater Ave atque Vale'—as we wander'd to and fro
Gazing at the Lydian laughter of the Garda-lake below
Sweet Catullus's all-but-island, olive-silvery Sirmio!

Thomas Hardy   *From the painting in the National Portrait Gallery*

TWELVE

Thomas Hardy
(*1840-1928*)

Thomas Hardy liked to remember that two peculiar things had happened to him when he was a baby. First, when he was born, in a thatched cottage under the black heathland of Dorset, at Stinsford, on June 2, 1840, at eight o'clock in the morning, the doctor thought him dead and threw him aside. And he might have been left to die if the village nurse had not picked him up and cried out that his heart was beating and that he wasn't dead after all.

Then, as he slept in his cradle one day in that first summer, an adder (or perhaps it was really a harmless grass-snake?) somehow found its way indoors, and into the cradle, where it curled on top of him and went to sleep on his warmth.

I suppose Hardy knew that the snake (which is why a snake coils round the staff of Aesculapius, the god of doctors) was a symbol of ancient wisdom. The baby grew into a small, wise, energetic man with a Dorset accent, who thought much in his long life (mostly a Dorset life) about love and men and women and fate and death and a God—supposing God existed—who seemed to him to have made rather a poor job of a world for mortals to live in.

Hardy was not really so poor as a lonely, thatched cottage

may suggest. The cottage was one of a small hamlet in Stins
ford parish, away from the main road. There his father had a
mason's business, and money enough to send Hardy to a
school a few miles off in Dorchester, and later on to place
him with an architect.

Architecture, one better than mason's work or building, wa
to be his way of earning. He did not become a poet all a
once, or write poems, as many poets have done, when he wa
small. But he learned to read very early, and, like a good many
other poets, he took to music. Just as John Clare learned the
violin from the gypsies, so Thomas Hardy learned it from hi
father, the builder and mason, who used to play airs and jig
and hornpipes and reels and waltzes on his violin at home in
the evening. On Sundays he also played the bass-viol as one
of the little orchestra or band of music-men who provided the
music in the parish church (this was commonly done in coun
try churches in the last century).

When Hardy was learning to be an architect in a Dorchester
office, he still used to go around in the evenings with his fa
ther to play the violin at dances, socials, and weddings in the
villages and farmhouses.

The first poem by himself that he remembered, the first he
kept, was a most clear description of the cottage he lived in
with his father and mother and his three sisters. He forgot
exactly when he wrote this imitation of Wordsworth, but it
was between seventeen and twenty.

As it turned out, novels were the first things he published,
though poems were the last—as well as the first—things he
wrote. It was his poems he most liked (though his novels
made him famous) and hoped to be remembered by, though
many, many years went by before they appeared in print.
Poems he made when he was twenty-five, twenty-six, and
twenty-seven he sent around to magazines. They were not at
all what editors thought poems should be. They were not

ugary, they were not written in poetry-language, and none of them were accepted. Hardy was not discouraged for long, and many years after he wrote that probably the editors "did not know good poetry from bad." To tell the truth, that is always the way of editors. Most of them choose only by fashion.

All the while, indeed all his life, Hardy was seeing strange things, which he remembered and thought about. Here is a peculiarity about poets and painters. The actual things they experience are not, after all, so very "strange." Others can see them, hear them, feel them, sense them as well. Either they do not notice them, or they sense them just in passing, do not think about them, and forget them. The poet's senses are more open: he sees, and he remembers. The thing caught by his senses becomes more than a sensation, it becomes an experience. The poet hoards his experience. And he may wonder about it, may ask—as Hardy was always asking—"Why?"

In the cottage in Stinsford parish his father had painted the stairway wall Venetian red. The cottage faced the sunset, and when the sun came in, it made a great evening blood-glowing brilliance of this color. Hardy remembered how when he was small he would wait by the stairs to see it, and would then say to himself, from a hymn: "And now another day is done."

Always he was encountering passings away of that kind, or deaths of one kind or another. While he was learning his profession, he was home one morning when, at eight o'clock, a murderer was to be hanged in Dorchester. He climbed a hill on the black heath behind the cottage and put the large brass-bound family telescope to his eye, directed it toward Dorchester and the prison, and then, at that very moment, within the round of the telescope he could see the murderer in white fustian under the gallows—"the white figure dropped downwards, and the faint note of the town clock struck eight."

He wrote of himself that he "seemed alone on the heath with

the hanged man, and crept homeward wishing he had not been so curious."

Another experience of mortality which Hardy did not forget fell to him in London, the job of superintending the removal of the ancient dead when the railway was driven through the old churchyard of St. Pancras. Behind a billboard, by the flare of gas lights, Hardy watched men carrying away the still knit together skeletons on planks.

The hanged man in the telescope and each skeleton on its plank again made Hardy ask why, why, and again why, about death and life (all death, all life, whereas Tennyson had asked questions about Tennyson). He said that his own life was to be a science of emotion, not a science of social climbing; and it was after his return from London to Dorset that Hardy had the great experience of all his years, out of which, in part, he made his greatest poems. It was in 1870 (Hardy was now twenty-nine). On a Monday morning in March, in his father's house, he rose at four o'clock, the stars still shining, and set out on a journey to North Cornwall, a hundred miles away, across Dorset, across Devonshire, to St. Juliot, on the sheer Atlantic cliffs. His mission was to see about restoring St. Juliot Church. The train took him to Launceston. There he hired a trap to carry him sixteen miles to the rectory.

He arrived in the dark, and knocked—and the first person he saw by lamplight was a tall, rather flustered girl, with blonde or nut-colored hair above her paling and flushing cheeks and her large gray eyes. This was Emma Gifford, whose sister was at that moment upstairs with her husband, the rector, who was ill in bed. She noticed Hardy's beard and his soft Dorset accent, and thought the blue paper sticking out of his pocket was a plan of the church, though really it was a poem.

Hardy fell in love, so did she; and when he came back he seemed to his sisters and his parents filled with that "radiance

are and fathomless" he mentions in the poem he wrote then
and there—"When I Set Out for Lyonnesse" (page 169)
—Lyonnesse being Cornwall.

It was four years before they were married, years in which
Hardy made the Lyonnesse journey several times, years in
which Hardy and Emma had picnics together on the cliffs,
picked primroses and orchids, listened to the Atlantic down
below, watched the seals, and stared into Atlantic sunsets.

After a while, though Hardy's novels had made him famous
through the world, his wife took to thinking that she had married beneath herself, and that Hardy was her inferior, so
their marriage in their Victorian house outside Dorchester became one of coldness and unhappiness. In poems he asked
why—why love had to change, why even love couldn't justify
the world. Then—they were both old—Emma Hardy died, in
1912. After she had been buried among the Hardys in Stinsford churchyard, under a yew, Hardy read some pieces of au-
tobiography she had written, including a description of their
first meeting and of the windy, sunny, rainy years of their
courtship above the Atlantic. On March 7, 1913, this old little
man of seventy-two, frail but very strong in mind and feeling, arrived again at St. Juliot, which he had first seen on
March 7, 1870. After that first journey he had written "When
I Set Out for Lyonnesse." Now after this other journey, forty-
three years later, he wrote love poems about Emma Hardy,
Emma Gifford, as she had been, on the cliffs, when she was

> all aglow
> And not the thin ghost that I now frailly follow

—love poems forty-three years after the first flush of their being in love, in which he was inclined to sweep away everything, every disappointment, every doubt and rejection of the
gray fate of men, in recollection of how much he had loved
her.

Hardy wrote down that he had been a slow developer in his strength, a child until he was sixteen, a youth until he was twenty-five, a young man until he was nearly fifty. Some poets only write well when they are on either side of twenty, as we have seen. Hardy still had poems to write, tender, moving, still "modern"-seeming poems, when he was eighty, and even older.

When, an old, old man of eighty-eight, he died at last in 1928, after forgiving whoever seemed responsible for the world and for the existence of men, they overruled his wish to be buried with his wife in the churchyard at Stinsford. Instead his ashes were a little grandiosely interred in Westminster Abbey, a burial place which may have suited Dryden or Tennyson, but which scarcely suited this rejector of pomp and circumstance. But his heart was taken out of his body, and placed in his wife's grave.

All through his life this poet felt that a stone doorstep worn by human feet was more to him than mists or mountains. Little known to himself, he became the master, when he died, of young poets in England and America.

WHEN I SET OUT FOR LYONNESSE

When I set out for Lyonnesse,
    A hundred miles away,
    The rime was on the spray,
And starlight lit my lonesomeness
When I set out for Lyonnesse
    A hundred miles away.

What should bechance at Lyonnesse
    While I should sojourn there
    No prophet durst declare,
Nor did the wisest wizard guess
What would bechance at Lyonnesse
    While I should sojourn there.

When I came back from Lyonnessee
    With magic in my eyes,
    All marked with mute surmise
My radiance rare and fathomless,
When I came back from Lyonnesse
    With magic in my eyes!

A THUNDERSTORM IN TOWN

She wore a new 'terra-cotta' dress,
And we stayed, because of the pelting storm,
Within the hansom's dry recess,
Though the horse had stopped; yea, motionless
    We sat on, snug and warm.

Then the downpour ceased, to my sharp sad pain
And the glass that had screened our forms before
Flew up, and out she sprang to her door:
I should have kissed her if the rain
    Had lasted a minute more.

THE VOICE

Woman much missed, how you call to me, call to me,
Saying that now you are not as you were
When you had changed from the one who was all to me,
But as at first, when our day was fair.

Can it be you that I hear? Let me view you, then,
Standing as when I drew near to the town
Where you would wait for me: yes, as I knew you then,
Even to the original air-blue gown!

Or is it only the breeze, in its listlessness
Travelling across the wet mead to me here,
You being ever dissolved to existlessness,
Heard no more again far or near?

    Thus I: faltering forward,
    Leaves around me falling,
Wind oozing thin through the thorn from norward,
    And the woman calling.

LYING AWAKE

You, Morningtide Star, now are steady-eyed, over the east,
    I know it as if I saw you;
You, Beeches, engrave on the sky your thin twigs, even the
     least;
    Had I paper and pencil I'd draw you.

You, Meadow, are white with your counterpane cover of dew,
    I see it as if I were there;
You, Churchyard, are lightening faint from the shade of the
     yew,
    The names creeping out everywhere.

THE GARDEN SEAT

Its former green is blue and thin,
And its once firm legs sink in and in;
Soon it will break down unaware,
Soon it will break down unaware.

At night when reddest flowers are black
Those who once sat thereon come back;
Quite a row of them sitting there,
Quite a row of them sitting there.

With them the seat does not break down,
Nor winter freeze them, nor floods drown,
For they are as light as upper air,
They are as light as upper air!

AFTERWARDS

When the Present has latched its postern behind my tremulous
    stay,
    And the May month flaps its glad green leaves like wings,
Delicate-filmed as new-spun silk, will the neighbours say,
    'He was a man who used to notice such things'?

If it be in the dusk when, like an eyelid's soundless blink,
    The dewfall hawk comes crossing the shades to alight
Upon the wind-warped upland thorn, a gazer may think,
    'To him this must have been a familiar sight.'

If I pass during some nocturnal blackness, mothy and warm,
    When the hedgehog travels furtively over the lawn,
One may say, 'He strove that such innocent creatures should
    come to no harm,
    But he could do little for them; and now he is gone.'

If, when hearing that I have been stilled at last, they stand at
    the door,
    Watching the full-starred heavens that winter sees,
Will this thought rise on those who will meet my face no more,
    'He was one who had an eye for such mysteries'?

And will any say when my bell of quittance is heard in the
    gloom,
    And a crossing breeze cuts a pause in its outrollings,
Till they rise again, as they were a new bell's boom,
    'He hears it not now, but used to notice such things'?

IF YOU HAD KNOWN

If you had known
When listening with her to the far-down moan
Of the white-selvaged and empurpled sea,
And rain came on that did not hinder talk,
Or damp your flashing facile gaiety
In turning home, despite the slow wet walk
By crooked ways, and over stiles of stone;
If you had known

You would lay roses,
Fifty years thence, on her monument, that discloses
Its graying shape upon the luxuriant green;
Fifty years thence to an hour, by chance led there,
What might have moved you?—yea, had you foreseen
That on the tomb of the selfsame one, gone where
The dawn of every day is as the close is,
You would lay roses!

WHERE THE POEMS
COME FROM

Three dots (. . .) indicate an extract from a longer poem. Where the name of the poem is given (*"From* 'The Lie,' " *"From* 'The Anniversary,' " and so on) there will be no difficulty in finding the complete poem in the poet's collected works in any library.

The following list will enable you to hunt down other extracts:

John Milton

Page 53. "Now Came Still Evening On," from *Paradise Lost,* IV, 598-609.

Page 54. "Eve to Adam," *ibid.,* 639-656.

Page 55. "After the Death of Samson," from *Samson Agonistes,* 1708—.

John Dryden

Page 82. "Zimri," from "Absalom and Achitophel."

Page 83. "The Poet Thomas Shadwell," from "Macflecknoe."

Page 84. "Fools in England," from "Epilogue to The Husband his own Cuckold."

Page 84. "At Nature's Early Birth," from "Juvenal's Sixth Satire."

Page 85. "The Flood," from "The First Book of Ovid's Metamorphoses."

Page 86. "All, All of a Piece Throughout," from "The Secular Masque."

Page 87. "Whom Death has Doomed," from "Lucretius, Against the Fear of Death."

Christopher Smart

Page 96. "Christmas Day," from "The Nativity of Our Lord and Saviour Jesus Christ."

Page 97. "The Saints Unknown," from "All Saints."

Page 98. "Prayer and Praise," from "St. Philip and St. James."

William Wordsworth

Page 128. "All Things That Love the Sun," from *Resolution and Independence.*

John Clare

"The Puddock's Nest" (page 140) and "The Cuckoo" (page 141) are taken from Clare's manuscripts.

The poems by Thomas Hardy on pages 169–172 are reprinted by permission of the Trustees of the Hardy Estate and Macmillan & Co. "Lying Awake" is reprinted from *Collected Poems* by Thomas Hardy; copyright 1928 by Florence E. Hardy and Sidney E. Cockerell, renewed 1953 by Lloyds Bank, Ltd. "When I Set Out for Lyonnesse," "Thunderstorm in Town," "The Voice," "The Garden Seat," and "Afterwards" are reprinted from *Collected Poems* by Thomas Hardy; copyright 1925 by The Macmillan Company.